# Please Don't Piss on the Petunias

To Jessica,
I heard you have chickens – and a garden! ♡
I hope my book will give you some laughs and some pointers.
XO
Sandra Knarf

Published by Greenwoman Publishing, LLC
Colorado Springs, Colorado
greenwomanpublishing.com

This book is a memoir. It reflects the author's recollections of experiences over a period of time. Some names and details have been changed, some events have been compressed, and dialogue has been recreated.

All brand names and product names used in this book are trademarks, registered trademarks, or trade names of their respective holders. Greenwoman Publishing, LLC is not associated with any product or vendor in this book.

Printed in the United States of America

First Edition: January 2019

Selected chapters in this work were previously published, in different form, in the following: *Greenwoman Magazine, Greenwoman Zine, US Represented, GreenPrints, MaryJanesFarm* Magazine, and *Flora's Forum*. Other chapters were read on KRCC (NPR's Southern Colorado affiliate station) radio program "Western Skies."

Publisher's Cataloging-in-Publication Data
Names: Knauf, Sandra, author.
Title: Please don't piss on the petunias: stories about raising kids, crops, and critters in the city / Sandra Knauf.
Description: Colorado Springs, CO: Greenwoman Publishing, LLC, 2018.
Identifiers: LCCN 2018911427 | ISBN 978-0-9905385-6-1 (pbk.) | 978-0-9905385-7-8 (eBook)
Subjects: LCSH Knauf, Sandra. | Gardening--Colorado. | Pets. | Parenting. | Urban agriculture. | Gardeners. | BISAC GARDENING / Regional / West (AK, CA, CO, HI, ID, MT, NV, UT, WY) | PETS / Essays & Narratives | FAMILY & RELATIONSHIPS / General Classification: LCC SB453.2.C6 .K63 2018 | DDC 635/.09788---dc23

# Other Titles by Greenwoman Publishing

*Zera and the Green Man* by Sandra Knauf
*Greenwoman Volumes 1-6* by Various contributors
*Fifty Shades of Green* by Various authors

*To Andy*

# Please Don't Piss on the Petunias

## Stories About Raising Kids, Crops & Critters in the City

# Sandra Knauf

Colorado Springs, Colorado

# Table of Contents

# Introduction

As a typical American kid with baby boomer parents, I yearned for two things — plants and animals. My siblings and I grew up in suburban-style homes with cookie-cutter landscapes made up of bluegrass lawns and a few standard-issue shrubs and trees. Our parents, who worked outside the home and had the responsibilities of providing for up to six kids (depending on the year and the household, as there were two) were not interested in indulging in pets.

I knew my life would be different when I grew up.

These are the stories of different — how my husband Andy and I brought up our two daughters, Zora and Lily, in an urban paradise filled with plants and pets, adventures and misadventures, and a daily dose of chaos.

We started out simply, with one dog and one cat. As I was the ringleader in this country-in-the-city experiment, I introduced the girls to more animals gradually — first taking Zora, as a kindergartener, to the pet store and letting her select and name the fish for a new aquarium. A little later, when she was seven and her little sister Lily four, I became obsessed with the idea of raising chickens. The girls and I visited a feed store one morning and walked out with a half-dozen exotic breed bantam chicks. What followed that summer was one of the most memorable experiences of their childhood and my life, and the genesis of this book. Always the supportive spouse, Andy not only put up with my wild and woolly ideas when it came to child rearing, gardening, and animal raising, but helped me when I needed help and encouraged me to live my dream.

Through the years we enlarged our gardens and our menagerie. We thrilled at the beautiful songs of a yellow-tufted canary named Elvis (given to us by a neighbor as a rescue bird), and we adopted a

Dalmatian that Zora named Alice, after *Alice in Wonderland*. We bought pet store goldfish for our hand-dug pond and the girls played with dwarf Netherlands rabbits. I took the girls with me to garden club meetings, plant nurseries, and state fairs; together we learned about honeybees and butterflies, flowers, fruits, shrubs, and trees.

By the end of their childhood, our daughters learned not to scream at hairy jumping spiders with fluorescent green fangs but to open a book and find out more about them. Those years, spent nurturing baby chicks and ducklings, rabbits, puppies, kittens, plants, and more taught them firsthand about life and death. Nature was their homeschool, and with every new experience, their world (and ours, as parents) grew a little bigger, more beautiful, more understandable, and, paradoxically, more mysterious.

We learned that living a life outside of the mainstream could be tough and frustrating at times but rewarding on a level that we never imagined. I hope you'll enjoy this collection of stories that I wrote over those years and that you'll find encouragement in them to live the life of *your* choosing.

# Eight Years to a Garden

*"The soul must be fed; we must have inspiration from stars, and sun beams, and flowers . . ."*
— Shirley Hibbard

A few hours before closing, we visited the dilapidated Victorian house one more time. In tears, I asked Andy for reassurance. Buying this place had been my idea. We'd been renting for years, and I had pushed for us to get something, anything, we could own.

As a young married couple with low-paying jobs (I worked as a secretary, Andy in construction) we cared about only two things — that the property was affordable and that it had potential. The potential was there, as the house had good square footage: five small rooms downstairs, including an enclosed porch/pantry, and two rooms upstairs under the eaves. Unfortunately, it had no land, only a few square feet of dirt between the front porch and sidewalk. This was disappointing as I had wanted to garden since I was a teen. But, there was promise: a big vacant lot next door that we hoped to purchase as soon as we got back on our feet financially.

Due to its sorry state, this house was the cheapest place on the market in our neighborhood. We calculated that we could make payments on it even if one of us lost our job. As if to test us on that point, a week earlier and right before Christmas, Andy had been laid off at the HVAC company where he'd been working for five years.

As we stood in the kitchen, looking at Pikes Peak through the small window over the filthy, rusted sink, I asked, "Are you going to wind up hating me for this?"

"Don't worry," Andy said. "We'll stay afloat, we'll make it work."

We signed the papers that day, for a house that had been on the market for well over a year and was so dirty and disgusting that my

1

mom said she cried after her first visit. Mom was no stranger to exaggerated statements, but this was not one of them. Andy and I had made jokes about how it was a "Westside charmer" and an "Old Colorado City fixer-upper," real estate euphemisms for dumps in our historically-important-yet-rundown neighborhood. We weren't laughing now.

* * *

Several days later, on a freezing cold Friday night, we (me, my little sister Karen, and her childhood friend Kiawa, all of us 20-somethings) painted over the wall grime in the two front rooms. While we worked downstairs, Andy ripped out filthy orange shag carpeting upstairs.

As I reloaded my paint roller, Andy appeared again in the doorway leading to the upstairs. He had just dragged another rolled piece of carpeting down the narrow stairway.

"I've never seen anything like this," he said. "They hammered in about 10 nails every square foot!"

He hauled the carpet out the back door. I turned away, so as not to breathe in any of the dust.

The filth was truly remarkable. When we started cleaning that morning, we discovered that cockroaches and mice had taken over the kitchen. Grease and gunk covered the walls and appliances; garbage filled the closets and bedrooms. Andy found a diaper, filled with dried baby shit, above the archway separating the dining room and kitchen.

Andy had shared a neighbor's tale about the previous owners. Allegedly, they once had a "gun battle" in the street. (I didn't ask for details. I didn't want to know.) That story, and the one about the dirty diaper, had been only two of the day's highlights. While tackling the kitchen filth, I discovered something Andy already knew about. As my sister, Karen, and I pushed the grease-covered Magic Chef stove away from the wall to tear out the linoleum, we uncovered a bed of cockroaches living on top of grease and mouse shit. I gagged and almost vomited.

Andy had watched from the doorway with a look of amusement. After I regained control, I yelled, "That's why you asked me to move this!" Andy chuckled, and I told him how much he sucked. Karen and Kiawa no doubt wondered what they had volunteered for, but (troopers that they were) they returned for a second round that night.

Kiawa had brought a six-pack of Coors, and Karen brought a bandana that she wore as a homemade dust mask. Perched on a ladder, she painted the ceiling, while I, wielding a long-handled paint roller, worked on the walls. In the front room, Kiawa painted around the window trim and doorway.

Andy had just returned upstairs for another go-around with the carpeting when the front door opened. Three teenaged girls, wearing heavy makeup and winter coats, one carrying a six-pack of Mickey's big mouths and the other a bottle in a brown paper bag, walked in.

The leader of the pack, a blonde with big hair and a denim coat, looked around at the three of us and demanded, "What are you doing here?"

I stared, speechless. Kiawa, small, dark-haired, and legendary in our family for her badass boldness, stalked over to them. "What the fuck are *you* doing here?"

"This is our party place," the leader declared.

My mouth dropped open in disbelief. Kiawa took another step toward them. The two girls behind the leader backed up a half-step.

While Karen and I stood transfixed, Kiawa let loose: "Who in the hell do you think you are, and what is wrong with you? Do you really think we're painting this place for you to *party* in? Can't you see this is these people's house?" As if any emphasis was needed, she stuck her paint brush up to the blonde's face. "Get your asses out of here — right now — and don't you ever come back!"

Without another word, the girls took off. As we all laughed uneasily and marveled over Kiawa's fierceness and the nerve of those girls, Andy came down to see what was going on. We told him, and he said, "Yeah, kids have been using the house as a party place for a long time. I cleaned out a few bags of beer bottles and garbage from the basement yesterday."

There used to be an organization called the "Welcome Wagon" where a neighborhood representative would visit new homeowners with glad tidings and a gift basket full of goodies. That was our Westside welcome wagon.

* * *

Almost eight years later, those early days came back as our two-and-a-half-year-old daughter Zora attempted (once again) to climb over the baby gate that blocked those steep and now-uncarpeted stairs. Our black Lab, Cato, was lying by the gate and she was trying to use him as a stepstool.

"Oh, no, you don't." I snatched her up and gave her a kiss.

"But Minnie's up there."

"I'll get Minnie, honey, right after we get you dressed. But you do not go upstairs by yourself."

"Okay, Mommy." Zora gave me a smile, I gave her another kiss, and we went into the living room where I dressed her in her Barney the dinosaur T-shirt, floral leggings, and pink Velcro sneakers. After lunch, on this beautiful October day, we'd head down to our new home, which was under renovation just 10 blocks away.

Andy and I had accomplished a lot in eight years: starting a business (Andy was now a licensed contractor); finishing college (I finally completed my BA in English after years of going part-time); investing in and beginning renovation on a second property with a friend (a house that was even a worse wreck than this one had been and had cost only nine thousand dollars); and, most meaningfully, becoming parents — first Zora, and another baby due in less than a month.

It'd taken years, but we'd renovated the small Victorian, top to bottom — on a less-than-a-shoestring budget, with no outside help and no loans. The year we moved in, we discovered a turn-of-the-century mansion downtown slated for demolition. We tore out oak flooring, old glass-fronted kitchen cabinets, and wainscoting and reinstalled them in our new home. From a commercial building Andy found decorative tin ceiling that we repurposed. Through the years and bit by bit, we kept at it; we might not have made a sow's ear into a silk purse, but we transformed a "dump" into a comfortable, and even charming, home.

The only thing we still lacked was outdoor space. Two years after we moved in, the vacant lot to the east of us was snatched up by the middle-aged neighbor on the other side (who had heard Andy express the desire to buy it). He promptly built an ugly three-car garage as close to our property line as he could. It blocked the sun to the wrap-around porch, our only private outdoor space. Then he added a chain-link fence around the lot and moved in his two large and unpleasant dogs.

Becoming parents intensified the desire for a yard. It was more than wanting a place for Zora to play; with motherhood, my environmental awareness had bloomed. For the last two years, I'd been reading about organic farming, GMOs, and global warming — and the more I thought about our family's health and well-being, the more I wanted a place where we could connect with nature and grow some of our own food.

Then one day, when Zora and I were in a used bookstore, I came upon Bonnie Marranca's *American Garden Writing: An Anthology*. Through the essays of Thomas Jefferson, Alice Morse Earle, J. I. Rodale, Wendell Berry, Allen Lacy, Elizabeth Lawrence, Celia Thaxter, and others, a new dimension of environmentalism opened up. For years I'd been a freelance writer but had never found my topic. That day, in the genre of garden writing, I found my passion. The more I read, the greater the desire for a garden grew. It was time to get my hands into the soil, to connect firsthand, to learn.

So, when Andy told me about the bungalow for sale, a nicer home with a huge backyard and right next door to our second property, my heart leapt. Andy had met the owner shortly after buying the second house. It had been summer and he volunteered to mow her front lawn when he mowed ours. It became something he did for the rest of the season, as he felt it was the neighborly thing to do. Freda expressed her gratitude by sending Andy home with zucchini and tomatoes from her backyard garden. They had developed a friendship, and Andy was one of the first to learn her home was going on the market.

I cleaned up the lunch dishes while Zora sat at the dining room table, finishing the apple juice in her juice pack.

"Are you about ready?" I asked as I walked back into the room.

As soon as I saw her, I began to laugh. Zora had on her Minnie Mouse Halloween mask from the dollar store. She was drinking through a straw sticking in Minnie's nose.

"Girl, you are something else," I said. "Do you have your doll? We need to get your sweater, too; it's almost time to go to the new house."

Zora released the straw, pulled up her mask, and grabbed her constant companion from her lap. She held it up to show me. "Minnie's ready."

\* \* \*

The day Andy told me Freda was moving to New York, my mom and I drove by to take a look at the house.

"It's pretty run-down," Mom said.

I looked at the place with her eyes: a plain one-story house (brown paint with faded and chipped yellow trim), a weed-filled yard, a sagging front porch stacked with boxes and other junk (the m.o. of a major hoarder). I thought, *Well, maybe it is, but I'm still excited to check it out!*

Sometimes in life, looks really are deceiving. There are people and there are houses that at first glance aren't thrilling — but when you take the time to explore further, you discover something extraordinary. Andy and I made an appointment to visit the next day, and when I walked through the front door, my pulse raced. *Oh, my God,* I thought. *I love this house!* The 1922 interior was typical Craftsman-style, with big picture windows in the living room and the adjoining dining room. The living room also had two matching

6

awning windows above a brick fireplace. The wide opening from living room to dining room was flanked with built-in, glass-fronted bookcases, and the entire back wall in the dining room was taken with a built-in, glass-fronted buffet. The buffet's brass hardware matched the two original brass chandeliers, and the buffet's oak matched the flooring, which was laid out in 12-board-wide frames (oak boards laid in the opposite direction). The best part was that none of the woodwork had ever been painted.

The effect of it all, the rich wood, the brass fixtures, the coziness, was so inviting and so beautiful, my excitement plummeted at the thought that we might not be able to buy it. I whispered to Andy, "I don't want to see the rest of the house. If we don't get it, I'll be heartbroken."

We made an offer and held our breath. Two days later we learned Freda had accepted it. Our elation lasted only a moment. The bank informed us that with Andy's new business and my "unemployment," we didn't qualify for the modest loan. Shame reared its ugly head: *This place is too good for you. Your hopes were too high. Maybe if you had a "real job . . ."* Then, unexpectedly, Freda — forever-after known to us as "The Angel" — decided to help us. She would carry our loan for a year, giving us time to establish credit-worthiness with a bank.

\* \* \*

Little did I know that this house-dream-come-true would signal one of the toughest years in our marriage. Andy had been working seven days a week, running his HVAC business and renovating the bungalow (as most of the house had not been updated since it was built in 1922). It made sense to do this now instead of waiting, but Andy's relentless work schedule, along with paying mortgages on two houses, my student loan, and a baby on the way, proved stressful beyond anything we'd imagined.

I'd been working keeping the home front together — running the office, taking care of Zora and Andy, and creating a new human. As usual, I fretted. As usual, Andy reassured me, "Don't worry. We'll make it work."

On that sunny October day, at age 32 and eight months pregnant, I was excited to be doing something I'd never done before. It would be my first big contribution to the new house: I was going to plant spring bulbs, two hundred to be exact. My sister-in-law Victoria, who worked for the city as a horticulturalist and was married to Andy's brother Danny, said she'd meet me at the house to give me some pointers.

Victoria was our gardening angel. That April she had met me at the property and identified plants: the bright orange poppies that were ubiquitous in our Old Colorado City neighborhood, two clumps of iris, a clump of asparagus, antique roses along one side of the one-car garage, spearmint right outside the back-porch door, comfrey, and volunteer garlic here and there and everywhere. A couple of times that summer, she'd dropped by and surprised us by weeding the front beds, removing wild bellflowers from the groundcover I'd learn was vinca. On another day, I'd arrived with Zora and Cato to find Victoria had planted snapdragons and dusty miller around a birdbath we'd placed in the center of the weedy backyard.

Aside from that pretty addition, the yard was a mess, but I was psyched. The spring next year would be gorgeous, and I would soon grow flowers, herbs, homegrown tomatoes, and whatever else I wanted.

\* \* \*

Victoria and Samantha, her four-year-old daughter, were on the front porch when we pulled up.

Samantha ran down the stairs and took Zora's hand. "We get to play on the porch while they plant bulbs!"

Zora held up her doll. "I brought Minnie!"

I asked about Samantha's big brother, "Is Alex here?"

"Andy's showing him something with the truck," said Victoria, "You know how he loves anything mechanical."

8

* * *

Victoria and I stood in the parkway, the strip of land between the sidewalk and the street. She thought this area would be a great spot for my one hundred daffodils.

She gestured, and I handed over the shovel. "I'll show you how we do it for the city," Victoria said. "We dig a big hole and plant a lot at once. It makes it so much easier."

She illustrated, swiftly spading out a two-foot circle of weeds/turf and then digging it out six inches deep. She moved with the grace and ease of someone who had done this many times before. Laying down the shovel, she got down on her knees and grabbed for the bag of bone meal. I joined her on the ground, with all the grace and elegance an eight-months-pregnant woman who had gained 40 pounds could muster.

Opening the bag, she said, "We sprinkle bone meal at the bottom, like so. This will be great food for them as they grow. Then you place the daffodil bulbs, pointy side up." I handed her a few from the big box, and she placed them. "You can put them pretty close," she added, "but don't let them touch; give them about an inch."

"Thank God you're here," I said. "I would have been digging a hole for each one!"

Victoria laughed. At work she grew and planted flowers, trees, and shrubs and cared for our city parks. My gardening guru, she took great joy in it all. For her, gardening was an easy pleasure. I, in contrast, was uptightness incarnate. The thought of planting bulbs (which had been a great extravagance, money-wise) had filled me with anxiety. I didn't want to screw anything up.

I scooped out another handful from the cardboard box. "What about these brown husks on the bulbs? They look like onion skins."

"Oh, those are their little jackets," said Victoria. "They'll help keep them warm this winter." *How sweet,* I thought, *"little jackets."* Our hands worked together, placing the bulbs in a circle, covering them.

Victoria stood, and I maneuvered to my feet with ungainly effort. "Now be sure to water them well," she said, "but don't step on the area until tomorrow or the next day. Give the soil time to settle; you don't want to compact it, as this is some pretty heavy clay. Just kind of tap it down a bit with your foot; get some of those air pockets out."

She grabbed the shovel again, and I protested, but she said she wanted to help me at least for a little while and wouldn't take no for an answer. I let her, thinking that maybe I'd calm down a bit if I saw her do it a couple more times.

"I can't thank you enough for coming by," I said after a few more holes. "This bulb-planting thing intimidates me."

"There's nothing to worry about, except planting them too shallowly. Then they could freeze. I planted bulbs with a group of schoolchildren once and they planted them too deep, upside down, sideways, you name it — and it was fine! They'll still come up, though they might take longer."

"Well, if small children can do it, so can I!" I said.

I told her about the bulbs I bought. The daffodils were 'Mount Hood,' an award-winning circa 1921 white heirloom. The rest were tulips, in pinks, greens, and purples. I'd selected 'Greenland,' which was "rose colored with soft green stripes from the flower's base to its tips"; and its "sport" (which meant a mutation that popped up), 'Green Wave,' a "parrot tulip," which meant it had fringed or wavy petals (this one had fringes). Another fancy tulip I'd splurged on was a peony flowering tulip by the name of 'Angelique' ("a scented beauty with graceful, double petals of pale rose with darker rose flushes and pale creamy-pink edges"). Accompanying the girly tulips was a purple one, 'Violet Beauty,' and the dark purple 'Queen of the Night.' I'd also bought 25 *Tulipa clusiana chrysantha*, a small naturalizing tulip, which was "vibrant yellow, flushed warm rose toward the petal edges." I had read it was one of author Henry Mitchell's all-time favorites.

"I know I went overboard," I said to Victoria. "I'm just so excited to garden."

"You'll have to come to my place next spring," she said. "I can give you some divisions from my perennials." Changing the subject, she asked, "Have you decided on names for the baby?"

"William if it's a boy, after my dad, and Lily if it's a girl."

"Lily's such a pretty name!" She paused. "Did you know tulips are in the lily family?"

I laughed. "You're kidding, right? Of course, I didn't know."

"The name is *Liliaceae*."

The Latin, like the English, sounded beautiful.

* * *

Two days before Thanksgiving, our Lily arrived — healthy, serene, beautiful, perfect. A week later, we moved into our new home, just in time for Christmas.

Getting there had taken eight long years, but it was worth it. I felt full and complete and giddy at the future opening up to us in this new home. I couldn't wait for spring.

# Mistress Gardeners

*Master Gardener: A person who has attended classes to learn everything there is to know about horticulture except what the person on the phone is asking.* (From "Master Gardener Definitions" handout)

A fiftyish Gloria Steinem look-alike interviewed me for the Master Gardener program. She and her sixty-something co-interviewer, also a woman, set me at ease with warm smiles, an offer of coffee, and good vibes.

Though my gardening expertise amounted to little more than a hill of beans, I wasn't nervous. My application had been filled out with as much earnestness and love as any. Under Question #2: "Why do you want to be a Master Gardener?" I began with a two-word answer, "personal enrichment," then rhapsodized shamelessly. I wrote of passion, of how my new garden, my first, had become a vital part of my life. I described the magic of sharing green discoveries with my two young daughters. I mentioned garden writing, a genre I was "smitten with," and told of my growing fascination with organic gardening and heirloom plants. An actual quote: "I have a fascination with how gardening relates to society; how the love of beauty, industry, and the creativity of growing things can elevate the individual and our culture."

I fessed up, though, to my lack of experience, which consisted mainly of reading, daydreaming, and only three years of actual hands-in-the-dirt work. I'd read a lot, but my reading had been selective, focusing on art and history. In science, I was an ignoramus. Plant growth and nutrition, photosynthesis, reproduction, etc., existed in my mind only as fuzzy eighth grade biology reminiscences. Which one was the pistil and which the stamen again? It seemed "pistil" evoked penis (is that a pistil in your pocket?) — so it's the male part, right? Wrong.

13

My plant identification was elementary too. I could tell a dandelion from a daisy but had no clue of the difference between a pine and a spruce, or a hellebore from a hole in the wall. I had no flair for fancy gardener's Latin. Recently I'd tried it out, inquiring at a nursery if they had CALA-dee-ums (caladiums, correctly pronounced cal-A-dee-ums). The nursery woman didn't even try to stifle her snicker at my Southern-fried interpretation.

Now at the interview, the only question these ladies focused on was Question #6, which dealt with fulfilling the commitment to the program. Classes began soon and continued over three months, one day a week, beginning shortly after the winter solstice and ending after the vernal equinox, a detail I thought fitting.

"No classes can be missed," the non-Gloria lady emphasized. "We go over a lot of material in a day, and it can't be made up. If you think you may have a problem with that, you need to let us know now." It went without saying that the mother of a toddler and a preschooler was a risky choice.

"There won't be a problem," I said. "I work at home, and my husband, who's self-employed, will be home to watch the girls on Mondays." The non-Gloria lady watched me intently as I spoke, searching, I imagined, for signs of insincerity.

They went over the apprenticeship program, a minimum commitment of 65 hours in the local Colorado State University's Cooperative Extension office. Again, they made sure I understood: non-compliance was *not* an option. I would not pass the course if I did not apprentice. I reassured them. Again.

Near the end of the interview I couldn't help but gush about what inspired me to become a gardener in the first place, Victoria's cottage garden, a garden I'd first visited almost 15 years earlier, at age 19. "It was paradise," I said, my smile revealing true green madness. After I gave them a run-down of all the features I'd admired in that first garden I fell in love with, the silver-haired goddesses nodded and smiled.

The next day I found out I'd been accepted. My syllabus runneth over, with lessons on everything from the largest players, climate and soils, to the smallest — microbes. Everything from plant sex to pest management, backyard fruit to bugs — even a dissecting microscope practice. Just reading the list of several dozen topics thrilled me. All this for a measly 65 hours of apprenticeship during the spring and summer and a 50-dollar student fee.

\* \* \*

The first impression of my classmates the next Monday was — Holy Estrogen! Thirty-eight students, only four men. I slid into my chair, thinking, *It's all women, older women.* I was one of a few under 40, one of a few not dressed in khakis and a Lands End polo shirt. Thanks to self-described garden writing experts like Jerry Baker, "America's Master Gardener®,"* I assumed most Master Gardeners were male. "Master" led me on, too. As I looked around the room, filled with future Mistress Gardeners, a possibility bloomed. Visions of women and their secret plant-bonding abilities danced through my mind. *So, it's true*, I thought. *Women are the real horticulturists, the imaginary witches, the ones who seek plant knowledge and communion with the natural world!* I imagined my classmates' devotion and brilliance, their insatiable curiosities, at once coldly scientific and wonderfully mystical. I felt honored and humbled; I'd been accepted to study among a tribe of wise women.

The large meeting room where we'd spend the next 13 weeks didn't fit that romantic notion. Institutional, windowless, and lit by large panels of fluorescents, its only saving grace was a modest kitchen with three industrial-sized coffeemakers. And I saw muffins. As I took it all in, beaming along with the rest of the initiates, the blonde woman sitting next to me introduced herself and asked what brought me to the program. Out I gushed again, telling her of my love of gardening and garden writing. The trim, 50-something woman had never heard of the genre.

"My husband and I just built our retirement home," she shared, naming a new, expensive community on the western foothills of our city, "and I wanted to learn about landscaping. I thought I could save a lot of money if I did it myself."

15

A plump, red-haired woman sitting across from us joined in. "We've been out in The Forest for a couple of years, since my husband's retirement, and we have five acres of pine trees to deal with!"

"The Forest" was another pricey area. There were probably as many horses there as two-leggers.

The women chatted about their landscaping challenges. The blonde mentioned how "the Mexican landscapers" had made some mistakes, due to the fact that "they could barely speak English."

*Okay,* I thought, *perhaps these ladies aren't exactly who I imagined.*

Virginia, a platinum-haired beauty with the modest title of Horticultural Agent, headed the Colorado Springs office. She welcomed us and told us the history of CSU's Extension program, which began in 1862 with the Morill Act. We learned about Land Grant Universities (like CSU), which originally taught agriculture and the mechanical arts, and we learned about the Hatch Act which created Agricultural Experiment Stations that conducted research. Eventually, services were offered at the county levels (Extension Office Services). These included: Agriculture and Natural Resources, Consumer and Family (home economics, 4-H programs), and Nutrition and Horticulture (including plant and pest management and the green industry). All had one main function, to get research-based information into our communities. Master Gardeners focused on helping homeowners with landscaping and gardening questions.

Virginia introduced Pete, the Plant & Pest Management Technical Specialist, and Lissy, the Administrative Assistant; together, they were the only full-time employees.

We learned that we'd have a new crop of instructors each week. They'd sit at a table on the other side of the room with prior students — Master Gardeners who wished to brush up on their knowledge or who were studying for Advanced Master Gardener Certification Level IV.

Virginia stressed that everything we were about to learn was "research-based knowledge" from CSU. She said the goal was not to memorize everything but to know where to find the answers. We'd need to know how to diagnose an aspen disease, how to I.D. a spider, what fruit trees were best suited for our climate, and anything else the client might ask relating to his or her landscape.

She then turned us over to Pete, the guy with the long title of "Plant & Pest Management Technical Specialist." He'd be our class supervisor.

"We're very happy to have you here," said Pete, a wizened, slightly built man in jeans and madras shirt. "This is a terrific class. You are going to learn a lot." Pete proceeded to energetically lay down the ground rules: don't miss any classes, be in your seat by 8:00 A.M., don't leave for lunch if you can help it, don't bring your kids to class. We'd have two 15-minute breaks per day, and a 45-minute lunch break. We'd probably never leave before 5:00 P.M., and only once in 20 years had the class been canceled because of snow. Then he gave us the vital victual info — while they'd provide hot water and coffee, and, for today only, the muffins, groups of three students would be responsible for the goodies each subsequent Monday. Please sign up at break. "I've found, through the years," Pete said, smiling slyly and then licking his lips, "that gardeners are the very best cooks." His suggestions for our morning table included baked goods (homemade went without saying) and fresh fruit.

Pete reminded me of a bantam rooster. As he laid down the law for the hens, I could almost see his rib cage expand, his walk turn into a strut. I knew he'd be keeping a sharp eye on us. As usual when it came to authority figures, I wasn't impressed.

Each of us took turns introducing ourselves. What I'd guessed was verified: the vast majority of the group held the esteemed position of white, middle class, middle-aged, educated woman. I fit in as a younger, more impoverished version. While about 11 students were from out of town and there for mostly educational reasons (one woman wanted to grow a windbreak on her eastern plains property, another wanted to work in another county's Extension Office), most were local. Of the rest, quite a few were transplants from other states who chose Colorado Springs as their retirement home, and, of these, the majority said they were taking the course as a means to learn how to landscape their properties. My dreamy idealism crumbled like rich brown compost. Cool undercover crones indeed! These modern sorceresses seemed more interested in conjuring pretty landscapes for their expensive homes than communing with nature. I'd heard Master Gardener certification was a status symbol; now I was seeing it.

Only a handful of us took the opportunity when introducing ourselves to profess obsessive plant love, including a woman from out of town who declared a joy for hand weeding. The room responded to that with a resounding "Eeewwww!" Pete grinned and said, "Yep, we always get one of those."

Another lover of the green, Chris, the pretty mom of a five-year-old boy, told her story. "My father was a gardener, and I never gardened when he was alive. I just wasn't interested at the time. Now, of course, I love it, and, well, I wish I could have shared it with him. . . ." At this point she teared up. So did we.

Several classmates stood out. While three of the four men were of Pete's generation, one was young, a handsome Cuban immigrant starting his own landscaping business. In a charming Ricky Ricardo accent, he shared that his wife was pregnant with their first child. We smiled and murmured congratulations, the yin energy so thick you could cut it with a Hori-Hori knife. Among the women, I noted with intrigue these standouts: a biologist from the city water plant, two semi-professional (read "close to poverty level") gardeners, and a journalist for a local paper.

The most eye-catching bloom in the bouquet sat at my table. Ivy was one of the two gardeners-for-hire, a waifish, wiry blonde with close-cropped hair and tattoos. She wore a leather jacket, jeans, and Doc Martens. I guessed this punkish forest-sprite to be in her late twenties. She didn't say much about herself.

The other stand-out female came from my zip code. Pete had passed out a list of our classmates and their addresses right before the introductions and I'd scanned it, imagining I'd find several students from my neighborhood to fraternize with since my working class/artsy/historic part of town had a lot of terrific gardens. Wrong again. There was one, a woman who looked a lot like Janis Joplin.

At her turn, Jade, with charming braggadocio, proclaimed herself a "house plant expert," saying she specialized in succulents and orchids and had won numerous blue ribbons at flower shows. She also told us about her exotic breed free range chickens, which she took on educational forays to elementary schools. She seemed to be trying to impress us with her great knowledge, and she succeeded, at least with me.

During a break, Ivy asked me, "So, how old are you?"

"Thirty-four."

"Oh," she said, "you look young too."

*Like you*, I thought. I smiled but didn't know quite what to make of her.

\* \* \*

That afternoon we started with weather and climate. The instructor, Gene, a fit, 60-something retired meteorologist for the Air Force, began by telling us, like Pete had, how lucky we were. "I was in one of the first programs, over 20 years ago, and it changed my life. This course influenced books I bought, friends I made, and lectures I attended. Some of the best teachers you'll ever have are in the room with you right now. And you will make life-long friends here." I looked around, wondering who they might be.

After the testimonial, Bob enlightened most of us on why Colorado Springs, at an altitude of 6,035 feet, was a bitch of a place to garden. Aside from a short growing season (148 days), a semi-arid climate (16.24 inches of rain average), and 30 – 40 degree drops in temperature during most 24-hour periods, there was also upslope, hail, and below-zero winter temperatures to contend with. We learned that our area was second only to Florida in frequency of lightning strikes. We also learned that Monument Ridge, which lies fifteen miles north of our city, had particularly severe winter weather and an accompanying oft-treacherous stretch of Interstate because it was the highest point between here and the North Pole.

"It's not that it's Zones 4 and 5 here," Bob said, "and it's not the coldness or, in particular, the dryness. It's all that combined with the winds. The winds literally suck the moisture out of plants. They are the single biggest stress factor."

One of the women sitting at the instructors' table motioned to Bob.

"Go ahead, Becky."

"I just wanted to say that I lived in Denver for several years and it was a lot easier to garden there," the attractive woman with long ash brown hair said. "Better soil, better weather, better climate."

"She's right," Bob said. "You wouldn't think it, Denver being just 60 miles to our north, but the growing conditions are a lot better there."

Becky gave Bob a wink and beamed at us. I'd noticed her earlier. She, like Jade and Ivy, seemed way out of the mainstream. She wore a broomstick skirt, floral shirt, metal and wood jewelry.

Bob ended by telling us we were in for a lot of fun — but needed to learn all we could so we could competently man the extension office. Silently, I changed that to "wo-man" the office.

"Just remember that of all the problems you'll see, most will not have a single cause and 80 to 90 percent will be abiotic, or not caused by a living organism. And you'll see plenty of problems. I guarantee you no one will walk in with a beautiful rose and say, 'Hey, I just wanted to show you this beautiful rose.' "

I chuckled along with the others, though I'd already learned enough in the first three hours to feel awestruck and intimidated. I couldn't stop thinking about it; so, it was the climate that made it so damn difficult for plants to flourish — and I just thought it was me!

\* \* \*

Each week we started the day by fueling ourselves on high-carb treats, such as bagels and flavored cream cheese with slices of cantaloupe, or cranberry-pistachio biscotti, crumb cake, and candied orange peel — and enough coffee to create a long line at the only ladies' room at every break. We'd begin our work with a quiz on what we'd covered the previous week then dig into the great garden of horticultural knowledge. Each Monday brought at least three different topics with at least three different instructors. Our handouts multiplied like earthworms in a rich compost pile, the information beginning to fill the three large three-ring binders Virginia told us to buy. Aside from the literature they gave out, there were book recommendations, such as the CSU-published *Household Insects*, *Woody Plants of the Pikes Peak Region*, and *Weeds of the West*; maverick writer/botanist Lauren Springer Ogden's *The Undaunted Garden*; and a library of others. For me, a book freak, many became must-haves.

When Pete did his class on soils, I learned that local types ranged from rock hard clay (my hood's "you-can-throw-a-pot-from-it" brand) to the north end's "decomposed granite," (sand). The ideal soil, a loam about two-fifths sand, two-fifths silt, and one-fifth clay, was virtually non-existent. It pleased me to learn that because clay is more nutrient-rich and holds water better, it's actually preferable to sandy soil. The complexities of soil, the myriad combinations of texture, structure, and chemical makeup, fascinated me.

We learned that if we were ever to become proper Master Gardeners, we'd stop using the "d" word. Pete told of a famous botanist who once flew into a rage when an assistant spoke the offensive noun, telling him, "*Dirt* is what is swept up from the floor!" It's *soil*, I reminded myself, lest my ignorance shine like the tiny bits of mica in a store-bought potting mix.

Each class day I found the green world more amazing, more humbling. We learned about the chemical mysteries of plant growth, the beauty and miracle of reproduction, and how to examine naked tree and shrub twigs to deduce the species through vascular bundle scars, leaf scars, and buds. We each held a mountain mahogany seed in our hand and learned the feathery white corkscrew curled and uncurled with humidity, working itself into the ground through the winter, planting itself.

In the Insect Class, taught by a youngish British man named Basil (who we all developed a slight crush on), we memorized 12 orders

21

of arthropods, plus non-insect anthropods (like spiders, which are arachnids, and pillbugs, which are crustaceans). We learned that an estimated eight million species in the creepy-crawly orders existed on earth, with an average of 7,222 new species described and identified annually. "Most are neutral, many are beneficial, and only a very few are harmful," Basil said.

The class giggled at Basil's description of the "googly-eye factor" in the general population's fear of bugs. We admired the gossamer wings of a dragonfly and saw tiny grasshoppers, just hatched in the dead of winter, from a plant sample. During one lesson we were asked to ID a cluster of one-sixteenth-of-an-inch-long, white cylinders, something we might be asked to do at the office. All of us decided that we were viewing insect eggs, what kind we weren't sure, but yes, they were definitely eggs. The Level IV Master Gardeners laughed at their trick — they'd given us grains of rice.

Pete sprang a surprise: we learned we had to turn in a bug collection. We'd have to seek out specimens from a minimum of eight orders, one per order, and we could include two additional non-insect samples (spiders, millipedes, etc.). When he saw some of our less-than-thrilled expressions, he clucked, "Remember, ladies, this year's collection is next year's teaching tool."

Pete described how to make a mini gas chamber by soaking a cotton ball in acetone and putting it in a jar. He said we could place an active bug in the freezer to make it slow down, go into hibernation mode — I guessed so they wouldn't try to get in a last-minute call to the governor. He gave us a handout on pinning them. I cringed, from my antennae to my ovipositor, and thought, *They didn't tell us this was part of the deal.*

"I don't know if I can do this," I whispered to a woman standing next to me at the microscope. "Do you think I could find enough that died by natural causes?"

"I'm going to pay the neighbor kids to do the work for me," she whispered back. "I'll offer 'em a quarter a bug."

I supposed I'd figure out how to deal with it, in the name of science.

We learned about tree abuse from Virginia, the Horticultural Agent. "The roots of a tree are usually shallow, and lateral," she told us. "It used to be, a long time ago, they thought that roots went down exactly like a mirror-image of the tree. But that's not so. While about 99 percent of the roots of a tree are in the upper three feet of soil, in clay loam, like ours, over 90 percent of those roots could be in the top 9 – 12 inches with most trees."

Murmurs of amazement filled the room.

"As we've learned previously, trees breathe through their roots as well as through their leaves, so you shouldn't put something like plastic or too much soil on top of them, especially in our dry climate."

I flashed on the only tree at our first home. It stood near the street, about 30 feet tall. I had no clue as to the species. It was none too healthy when we moved in (it even had a mailbox nailed to it), but by the time we moved, it was dead. I'd built my very first flower beds around that tree's base — beds 18 inches deep. I squirmed in my seat, imagining how I'd smothered those roots.

"And excavating can do a lot of damage," Virginia said.

I blushed, remembering the post holes we'd dug for our fence, how we'd hacked and chopped to get through some especially big, tough, stubborn roots.

I stopped listening to Virginia. I thought of the sidewalk and curb the city put in, our neighbor's ugly garage. We'd excavated the hell out of the area. The tree didn't stand a chance.

Guilty of tree murder, yet there I sat, pretty as you please, with Master Gardeners. I looked around, seeing if anyone noticed that I was a blatant fake, a pretender — kind of like those orchids that release a wasp-scented pheromone in order to get pollinated.

While I ate humble pie on more than several occasions, in some ways I was glad to be ignorant. I could soak it all up, like Pete's favorite (and, I'd later learn, ecologically controversial) soil enhancer, Canadian sphagnum peat moss. I was blissfully free from bias . . . almost free, anyway. I did harbor industrial-strength opinions on chemicals, Kentucky bluegrass lawns, and one or two other abominations. Otherwise, I was fairly open-minded.

Once we got into the -cides: pesticides, herbicides, fungicides, insecticides, and all other killers of Mother Nature, I saw a consensus of dissent. The majority of our class preferred organic controls. These ladies were old enough to have heard of Rachel Carson and smart enough to care. Even though we were told (several times) that the favored herbicide, Roundup, was both a great product and relatively safe to use, a few of us voiced our skepticism.

Virginia taught the thankless pesticides class and focused on the science. We learned the different chemical categories and how to read labels, and we examined figures on risk assessment and environmental losses. We poured over lists — pesticides discontinued since 1970, when the EPA came into being, and ones still in use today. Just the facts, ma'ams, and where, in the office, we could find almost-indecipherable-to-the-non-chemist reports and studies.

Everything we learned on this subject was frightening, dangerous, deadly. Our glossary handout included words to learn: *accumulation* – "the build-up of pesticides in the body of animals and man"; *LD 50* – "the dosage which will kill 50% of the test animals"; *mutagenic* – "can produce genetic change"; *non-target* – "any plant, animal or other organism that a pesticide application is not aimed at but may accidentally be injured by the chemical"; and *secondary pest* – "One problem is replaced by another new, previously unimportant pest, which multiplies rapidly in the absence of a competitor." What wasn't to love?

We also learned about IPM, or Integrated Pest Management, an improved philosophy defined as "Using multiple approaches to pest control." It was a system in which chemical, nonchemical, and cultivation practices were used together to combat a problem. Though it sounded more palatable than poison alone, it still reminded me of Elmer Fudd using a shotgun, dynamite, and a sabotaged carrot to get rid of the wascally wabbit. Bitterness overwhelmed me, so much that I segregated all pesticide information into a separate, unloved binder.

During this session, I realized that CSU received a lot of money, most of their research money, in fact, from places like Monsanto and Dow. The clue was all the literature and films with "Monsanto" or "Dow Corporation" somewhere in the fine, or not-so-fine, print. *Master Gardeners was directly linked to chemical companies*, I thought. Over and over we'd been told what we were learning was "unbiased and research-based," but how did that work, exactly, when corporate profit was involved? I felt like I just learned my husband was a mafia hit man.

I decided on premeditated environmentalism. For those clients who simply asked for help, I'd offer only non-chemical solutions; I would not condone any chemical treatments. If I faced consequences for my prejudice, so be it, they'd have one less Mistress Gardener.

Eight hours together in a room each week bred familiarity, and my classmates began to grow on me. The best part was their maturity — they were old enough to have had tried-and-true experiences and confident enough to know their minds and express their opinions. During the session on xeriscaping, or low water gardening, these attributes came out. The Utility Department's xeriscape representative, an attractive and petite blonde, presented a slide show featuring drought-tolerant grasses, vines, and other perennials, giving her assessment of each.

When a slide of ribbon grass (*Phalaris arundinacea* var. 'Picta') flashed on the screen and she labeled it invasive, Jade, the Janis Joplin look-alike/house plant expert/chicken lady, whispered, rather loudly, "Not if you don't water it."

William, the only male at our table, a sweet 60-something who'd waxed poetic about his terraced back yard, spring bulbs, and Egyptian walking onions, nodded in agreement.

When the xeriscape lady dissed silver lace vine as being "rather unattractive," both Jade and red-haired Rose muttered words equivalent to "bullshit."

"Silver lace is a great vine," Rose hissed. "It covers quickly, can get by on no additional water, and its flowers are pretty!"

"Where can I buy it?" I whispered.

She told me, adding instructions on stem propagation, which she said was easy. I jotted it down, knowing our behavior was not polite. But we didn't have a lot of free time. We spent most of our break time standing in line at the bathroom, and at lunch, after eating and making phone calls to work or home, we never got in enough gab. Each class day, Pete's cock-a-doodle refrain echoed, "It's time to get back in your seats, ladies."

In addition to chatting about children, grandchildren, cooking, and sometimes even gardening, other talk was predictably female. We thought the Cuban-American hunky, Basil the British-Bug-Guy attractive and droll, and we shared an envy of Ivy's waifishness, coupled with her ability to eat — a lot. She snacked all during class and once, as her leather-braceleted hand brought handfuls of peanuts to her mouth, Rose couldn't help herself. "That's a lot of fat; I don't see how you do it!"

"Hey, it's polyunsaturated," Ivy said. "Besides, I work it off!" Additional remarks were effectively lopped off by Ivy's sickle-sharp reply.

The weeks flew by, and soon my second-least-favorite subject came up: turf.

Turf, beloved turf, the biggest cash crop in Colorado (before marijuana became legal), bringing in billions over number two, that lesser crop with an actual purpose, wheat. Grass was the landscape choice of Colorado suburbia, a choice that sucked up 75% of our pure mountain water and created unending fertilizer and herbicide pollution. I groaned as we heard how lawns should be mowed twice weekly during their growing season for "optimum growth and beauty," how they should be given four fertilizer applications a year. Fertilize, water, mow, water, mow, water, mow, mow, mow. I couldn't help but whisper my own "bullshit." I wondered aloud if anyone with such a lawn actually had a life or any environmental knowledge.

To balance out anti-environmental subjects, we had Becky, a professional gardener, the president of a local garden club, the self-proclaimed compost expert, the most charismatic person in the room. Becky flirted with the men and treated all the ladies like girlfriends. I saw her paint her fingernails orange during one speaker's presentation, and she regularly made off-color quips about plant and insect sex, tree crotches, and the like.

Her lecture on composting and organic gardening, "Compost Happens," included concepts such as "party planting," or confusing insects with a mix of unrelated plants in the garden instead of placing like-species together, and "trap cropping," or drawing pests away from endangered plants with "decoy" plants. In a handout, *Beneficial Insects & Their Buddies*, bats landed in her "Too Cool to Categorize" section. She defined organic gardeners as "patient, tolerant, accepting of the hard facts of life, rewarded." She championed the environment at every turn, sharing information on permaculture, habitat creating, beekeeping, bird feeding, self-sufficiency. I dug her. She presented so much more than research-based information; she presented a *philosophy*.

At the time I was reading Michael Pollen's *Second Nature*. He also gardened with both mind and soul, and as I read chapters "Compost and its Moral Imperatives," and "The Idea of a Garden," I kept thinking, *Becky would like this*, or *this sounds like Becky*. I found another used copy (most of my books came from the used bookstore) and gave it to her. In return, she sent me a thank you card. On the inside, next to a doodled daffodil, was an invitation to join her garden club.

Although Pete had suggested on day one that we sit at a different table each week so we could meet everyone, we, of course, didn't. I moved two or three times, then settled near "my" group — Rose, Jade, Ivy, and sweet William. It would have been impossible to get to know anyone otherwise.

The women at my table made for a nosegay of opinions and experiences. The older ones' ages made them interesting perennials; they were established; they'd weathered seasons and developed strong, extensive root systems. During our lunch breaks, I learned a few things from Jade about keeping organically tended chickens, something I wanted to do, and how their eggs, with bright orange yolks, were nutritionally superior to anything available in a store. I also learned she'd survived cancer.

Rose, with the home in Black Forest, was brassy and tough, but she was cute and she knew her stuff. She said she was thinking of starting a gardening business and invited me to visit that spring and pick up a Nanking cherry shrub or two from the bundle of 50 she bought from the forestry department. She also knew plenty of sources for free composted horse manure. While she showed a tender, maternal side when talking about her teenage son, it didn't surprise me to learn this red-haired firecracker was once a weightlifter.

I learned Ivy worked at the summer home of a filthy-rich oil heiress who owned a gusher amount of prime real estate. Though Ivy was discreet, I glimpsed what she had to put up with.

"She allows only blue, white, and pink flowers," Ivy confided one day during lunch.

"You're kidding!" I knew the garden had a Victorian-inspired bedding scheme (very unimaginative in my opinion), but I couldn't fathom how one could live without stimulating, hummingbird-beloved reds, sunshiny yellows, dusky yet regal purples.

Ivy opened up her second bottle of orange juice. "One year we ordered a thousand lilies, and when they began to bloom, she decided the pink was a shade too dark. We pulled them all out, threw them in the dumpster."

I grimaced and thought of *Alice in Wonderland*'s Queen of Hearts and how the cards scrambled to paint the white rosebushes red. Off with their damned heads! That level of waste disgusted me.

When I learned Ivy earned little more than minimum wage and supplemented her hard work with bartending, I fumed.

William was listening in, enjoying his bologna on rye. "What a broad," he said, shaking his head.

Though I stuck with one table, I made it a point to chat with those who caught my interest: the journalist, the water plant engineer, the woman whose father was a gardener.

The journalist, Daphne, was a pleasant, quiet woman who seemed to go about life much as I did, speaking little and absorbing much. I discovered her husband was a doctor, and they always bought Douglas firs for their Christmas tree because his name was Douglas. She said her family used their dining room table for study and it was always covered with papers and books. I liked her.

Holly, the water plant engineer, had a degree in biology and loved organic gardening. She turned me on to an awesome catalog from a co-op out East, Fedco, that specialized in heirlooms and organic seed. She lived downtown. I liked her a lot, too.

I learned more about Chris, the woman whose father had been an avid gardener. She had a five-year-old son and we shared stories about our children. She told me of a Venus flytrap they'd had for well over a year, watered with tap water and thriving (flytrap instructions always say to use only distilled), about their new home near a rare wetlands area, and how they delighted in exploring the plants and wildlife.

Only one woman, Rue, annoyed me. Dressed to the nines each Monday, she made it a point to let us know she lived in a neighborhood that was not the wealthiest, but damn close to it. Many times I caught her eyeing the rest of us in a not-so-subtle "I'm determining your worth" way. Toward the end of the program, I heard her complain that her property was turned down for that summer's garden tour, put on by the wealthiest neighborhood's garden club. Rue declared, "I may not have a million-dollar house, but I have a million-dollar garden!" It was all I could do not to regurgitate, much like the common house fly.

\* \* \*

Too soon, we found ourselves at the last day of class. After a brief recap of the program's roots, we spent the morning learning office procedure for our mandatory 65 hours of volunteer work. The person who coached us was the Director of the program, Fen Miller. In from CSU at Fort Collins for the occasion, he was the only person we'd seen in a suit and tie. "Don't be afraid to ask a lot of questions. Don't be afraid to say you'd like to call them back after you do some research," Miller said. "Smile when you answer the phone — the client will hear that smile."

He told us we could send up to four S.I.A. (Service-In-Action) Bulletins to each client. They went from general information, like number .546 "Organic materials as nitrogen fertilizers," to specific, such as number 5.562 "Use of pheromones for insect control in Colorado."

"For walk-ins, don't hand out more than six sheets. If they want more, have them contact CSU. Let them know on-site visits are available for a fee, but most problems can be diagnosed over the phone. Keep asking questions until you're able to solve the problem. Fill out a call sheet on each call and be sure to try at least three times to get back with them. Our best role is to help facilitate informed choice," Mr. Miller said. "Let people know they are making the final decision."

I remembered the one time I'd called the extension. I wanted to buy a cherry tree and asked for a recommendation. The fellow on the phone, polite and helpful, had told me sweet cherries, like Bings, didn't do well in our climate. Soon I received a S.I.A. "Tree and shrub fruits for the Colorado High Plains." It listed sour cherry varieties, such as 'Meteor,' 'Van,' 'Black Tartarian,' and 'Montmorency,' and included information on planting and pollination. I'd been a satisfied customer. Soon, it would be my turn to help.

We toured the area where we'd spend our 65 hours, the cubicled corner of a large office. Pete's desk sat cubby-holed on one end, amid overhead and file cabinets. On our side was a small comprehensive library, tables, and two phones. Pete's space included the Master Gardener bulletin board, microscope area, colorful posters of flora, and his collection of insects and arachnids. He gleefully showed us his latest acquisition, a black widow spider, suspended in a small jar of alcohol.

"One of the students found that in her basement just this week." Pete grinned as a few students shuddered. I noticed the delicate paper wasp nest hanging by his desk and told him it looked like beautiful handmade paper.

"Yep, and it's really made from wood and wasp spit," Pete said.

We celebrated with a potluck lunch. The kitchen counters held a cornucopia of home cooking — casseroles, salads, home-baked bread, more desserts than you could sample. And for once we could socialize as much as we wanted. My husband and daughters came, and it was a big party. It all felt strange though, bitter-sweet strange, and an emotional quietness lay beneath our joviality. It was the first day of April, and I suddenly felt a little foolish. Looking at the ladies surrounding me in the chow line, I realized how far I'd come. Originally, in a bout of reverse-snobbism, I'd judged these ladies as being something quite less than dedicated horticulturists; now I realized we were all true lovers of the green. Only one person, an older gentleman, dropped out of the program, because of serious health reasons. Of the rest of us, not one missed a single day, a single hour. I'd also grown quite fond of arachnid-loving Pete.

Standing next to Becky in the chow line, I commented that a bean casserole looked particularly tasty.

"I'd better not," she said, moving a neon-pink-fingernailed hand towards the napkin stack. "I've got clients this afternoon, and I can't be tootin'."

Not five minutes later, after sitting down to eat, someone remarked on the deliciousness of the same dish.

"I wish I could have had some," the Cuban-American landscaper said, "but I've got to work this afternoon and I can't make any rude noises." He grinned slyly, just like Becky.

I grinned too. Yes, we were all the same, all peas-in-a-pod, us gardeners. All lovers of beans and earthy enough to comment on what beans do.

I sat there, eating, thinking. Thinking about how my world had grown. That very first day we were given a handout that read: "The subject of this course is HORTICULTURE — the science and art of growing plants." We were told to look at all the relationships and the impacts of all the various parts upon one another. To try to see the big picture.

I'd succeeded on that count. Never again would I hold soil in my hands and think of it as just dirt, never would I look at a tree, or a bug, or a flower in the same I'm-taking-it-all-for-granted way. Everything had become more alive through the winter, more mind-blowingly intricate, more connected, more in focus. I now noticed the shapes of individual trees, the geometry of a conifer needle, the number of petals on a flower, the markings on a spider. I had new eyes, and I was more in love than ever.

And I was forever humbled. One could spend a whole lifetime dedicated to collecting primroses, studying soils, or pondering the life of a honeybee, yet one could never hope to learn even a fraction of all there was to know! It felt wonderful to be close to Master Gardener status, and it felt silly, as I realized my ignorance more than ever before. Yes, we were the modern men and women of the soil. We were also the ones that it all had to be saved from. How could we ever proclaim ourselves masters or mistresses of something this grand?

# The Chicken Chronicles

Before I became a gardener, raising chickens seemed a throwback to the olden days, kind of like smoking your own hams or pounding your clothes on rocks down by the river. After I started gardening, it became my fantasy. It seemed the natural progression of things, going from cultivating plants to raising the animals that could provide their fertilizer. Ah, and what a picturesque fantasy! Chicken manure for the garden, fresh eggs, a sweet little henhouse with Martha Stewart charm in my very own urban backyard. It all began to be realized when I became friends with an elderly neighbor lady who raised bantam, or miniature breed, chickens. If she could do it, surely I could.

That winter Grandma Ruby and I hatched a plot. Ruby had two illegal roosters (roosters were banned in city limits) and four hens, and we decided that come spring, when her hens "went broody and began to set" (got it in their heads they wanted to become mamas and began to stay on a nest of fertilized eggs), we'd pull a switcheroo. I'd transport the maternal chicken to a shed Andy and I would convert into a hen house, along with a rooster for companionship, and then, in 21 short days . . . *voilà!* We'd have adorable, peeping, baby chicks running about. Perfect rustic bliss.

Late spring came, and we put our plan into action. One evening at dusk, I transported the chickens, in bushel baskets covered with worn bath towels, from Ruby's house to their recently renovated home. The chicken shack, as I called it, was clean, freshly painted, and nicely scented with pine-shaving litter strewn on the newly-poured concrete floor. Around the small yard in front, Andy had built a sturdy four-foot-tall wood and wire fence. Inside hung an old broomstick for a roost and a row of three covered nesting boxes. A straw-filled box for the broody hen sat on the floor.

As Andy and the girls watched, I gently placed the hen's toasty-warm eggs into the box. Then the birds, already named Deianeira and Hercules by seven-year-old Zora, were released. They were handsome chickens, about one-fourth the size of regular ones, with cream-colored heads and golden bodies.

The Lilliputian rooster with long, curved tail feathers, strutted his stuff, surveying his surroundings with a quick eye and elegant arrogance that could only come from a genuine cock-of-the-walk.

"He's a good-looking little guy, isn't he?" said Andy, smiling. I found this to be encouraging as he had not been thrilled with the scheme. Andy often, though not coming out and actually saying it, left me with the feeling that he thought my ideas were ill-conceived at best and crazy at worst.

The hen, not in a cheerful mood about her abduction and relocation, ignored the egg-filled nest on the floor and flew to one of the wall boxes. *That's okay,* I thought. *I'll just put the eggs under her there for now and then move her down to the floor when they're closer to hatching.* Deianeira pecked at me as I tried to slide the eggs under her. She then let out a screech of a curse and moved in a huff to an adjacent box. I understood perfectly: "I don't know *who* you are, but I don't like you!" After I filled the nest with her eggs, she decided she'd get back on them after all. I felt a small cluck of triumph as we closed the door on the coop for the night.

The first dilemma came the next morning. Aware that we were harboring a rooster, I spent most of the night anxious, worrying about the racket he'd make in the morning. Sunrise crowing was not a city value, hence the five *hen* limit. Andy and I awoke at dawn and looked at each other. Silence. "Great," I whispered, "maybe he isn't going to crow!" Ten minutes later, at exactly 5:20 A.M., Hercules began to announce the day. Now I didn't know if all bantams sounded like this, but this guy's crow was scratchy, hoarse, horrible, like someone with laryngitis, "UR-UR-UR-Uurrrr." It started out strong, then deteriorated to a deathbed gasp. It was nothing like the movies. I closed my eyes. *It's so loud!* I thought. *Maybe that'll be it, though.*

Andy and I hunkered down in the sheets and listened. Hercules didn't stop; he sounded the dawn alarm every few minutes, and every time, I cringed. We didn't know what could be done about it (besides murder), so after lying there awhile, wondering if and when it would ever stop, we got up. I made coffee and waited for the neighbors to come over and string us up. So, this was what mornings on the farm were like. "I didn't know it would be so *bad*," I said as I sipped my coffee, wincing at yet another cock-a-doodle-doo.

"I'm telling the neighbors it was your idea and I didn't have anything to do with it," replied my chivalrous mate. While we were both newly horrified every few minutes when we heard another fingernails-on-chalkboard salute, after a while we found ourselves grinning at our wickedness.

I had already decided, at 5:20 A.M., I would be taking Hercules back to Grandma Ruby's. We had agreed I could bring him back if his crowing was a problem, even though she didn't think it would be. She said her neighbors actually liked hearing the roosters. I wondered at that now.

A couple of hours later, after chasing the rooster around, trying to catch him, while Andy watched, laughing, and having the little guy get a small wound on his comb in the process (the rooster, that is), I finally cornered him, threw a towel over him, and put him in Ruby's basket.

I returned to Grandma Ruby's with the basket on my hip and a guilty heart that I had not only chickened out on keeping the rooster but had injured the beautiful, obnoxious bird. Ruby assured me he'd be okay, asked how the hen was doing (fine, still on her nest), and graciously took him back.

Back at home, we commenced waiting for the eggs to hatch. During this time, I tried to make friends with the hen. Several times a day I came in meekly, speaking in a soft and friendly tone, practically prostrating myself before the Queen of Eggs. I brought her the mixture of corn, millet, and other grains that they sell as scratch, plus a few treats, such as chopped up apples or greens. I tried to pet her. Every single time I came near she gave off outraged chicken vibes and pecked at my hand. She belonged to Grandma Ruby, no one else. She never left the nest in my presence. I never saw her eat. Only once I witnessed her off the nest. I heard the frantic, "BAUK! BAUK! BAUK! BAUUUK!" and raced outside to her rescue. There she was, running around the fenced area, still "bauking," feathers ruffled. I couldn't find the source of her terror, and my appearance didn't calm her any. After a few minutes I shut her back in the coop to quiet her. I worried that she might not return to the nest, but she did.

After 22 days, Ruby and I became concerned about the unhappy, solitary, (crazed, in my opinion) hen — that she'd spend all that time on her great task, and, as Ruby put it, "not have any babies." A few days before, I had moved her nest to the floor in preparation for the big event. She became more furious than I imagined possible. She raised her hackles (all the feathers down her neck) and actually looked like a *cobra*. She began pecking at me vigorously, defending her eggs, and in the process broke one of them. There was no chick in it — just the shrunken, jelled remains of what once had been. I was surprised it didn't smell bad. The next day, I noticed an egg I accidentally left in the wall box when moving the clutch. I took it outside, nervously opened it, and found it, too, was empty. Both the hen and I were depressed. She'd failed as a mama, and I'd failed as a chicken raiser.

* * *

The next day I called a feed store just south of our city. Now nearly July, I felt my time had been invested and I was determined to get chicks — one way or another. I inquired about ordering a couple of day-old bantam Silkies as a back-up plan, in case the hatching did not occur. The feed store lady lent a sympathetic ear as I bemoaned my situation. She said she'd call me back with a due date on ordering. Three days later the phone rang.

"Your Silkies are in," she said.

I caught my breath. "Oh, I didn't actually order them — I was just asking." Suddenly everything was happening too fast.

"I placed an order later that day and added a couple of Silkies, in case your eggs didn't hatch. It's okay if you don't want them; someone else will."

"Wait," I said, suddenly all aflutter, "I *do* want them. I'll be down in a couple of hours."

My daughters, patiently expecting along with me all this time, were as happy as I was — we were finally going to get chicks. The week before I had shown them a picture of Silkies. They are not your average looking chicken. Originating from the Far East, they were first mentioned by the Italian explorer Marco Polo when he wrote about them during his travels to China in the 13th century. Silkies are chickens whose feathers look like fur. You've heard of big hair, they have big "fur." My sister-in-law Amy calls them hippie chickens, but they look more like glam rock to me, the Ziggy Stardusts of chickens. They look this way because normal feathers have barbules along the barbs (the individual branches on a feather) that hold the barbs together, sort of like Velcro; Silkies lack these, so their barbs go out in all directions, giving the fur effect. They're very fluffy, from their feet to their topknots (the tuft of feathers atop their heads). They come in black, white, and buff, have unique black-toned skin, and have five toes, instead of the usual four. I thought they were very cool. Zora and Lily did not. When I asked if they'd like to have that type of chicken, they exclaimed in unison, "No! Those chickens look weird!" This burst my bubble, temporarily. Later, when I told my mom about their reaction, she said, "Don't worry. When they see them, they'll like them. *Trust me.*"

Once at the warehouse-sized feed store, we were directed to the back where a big stainless steel horse trough held a couple hundred active, peeping chicks. A parade of fluff danced before us — black chicks, white chicks, black and white, black and yellow, yellow, yellow with brown markings. There were bantams, about the size of a 50-cent piece, and regular sized chicks more than twice that big.

Baby chick acquisition greed swept over me. I quickly rationalized that since we were already there, and the chicks cost less than three dollars apiece, it would be ridiculous to leave with just two. I asked the feed store lady if there were "extras."

Zora, who always astonished me with her innate sense of style, which didn't seem to come, as far as I could tell, from either side of the family, fell in love at once with two big yellow chicks with brown speckles and stripes. They were full-size Araucanas, a South American breed that used to be advertised in the backs of old issues of *Organic Gardening* as the "Layers of Colored Easter Eggs." Martha Stewart raised them for their elegant turquoise blue- and green-shelled eggs. They were chic chicks. We were both disappointed to learn they were spoken for.

We decided to concentrate on bantams. The feed store owner scooped up my two white Silkies, who looked like fluffy white ordinary chicks except for their darker skin, and placed them in a small ventilated cardboard box. After some discussion, we settled on four more — two white and black chicks she called Golden Sebrights, a little black one with a yellow belly, and a yellow one that looked just like the kind you see in all the storybooks, except it had down-covered feet. With the latter two I forgot to ask the breed, and as bantams are too small to "sex" we didn't know how many would turn out to be hens and how many cockalorums.

On the drive home I felt giddy. The girls were too, and it came out in continual arguing over whose turn it was to hold the box. "Please be careful!" I pleaded repeatedly, my eyes darting to the rear-view mirror. Amid the mania, I silently hoped that the mother hen would accept them so I wouldn't have to take care of them.

At home again we went to the girl's playroom, formerly a small sleeping porch on the back of the house. A cardboard box with a 60-watt light clamped onto one side for heat would be the chicks' temporary home. We gave them food and water. Since I read it was best to wait until dusk to try to sneak them under the hen, we had a few more hours to enjoy them. Over this time we played hostesses to everyone we could find who might be interested in seeing them — our next door neighbors, the 11 year olds playing across the street, and a classmate of Zora's and her mother who happened by walking their dog. I figured if the hen accepted them, we wouldn't be allowed close contact, so we indulged to the fullest.

At dusk, I cuddled a Sebright chick next to me and took it into the hen house. The hen eyed me with her usual dislike. As I nervously slipped the fully alert chick under her she reacted immediately. But it was not with innate love for a new life. Instead, she turned and began pecking furiously at the chick — at its head. I screamed in horror and grabbed the trembling chick. She screamed. We screamed in unison. For several seconds, chaos reigned in the darkened coop. The whole scene would have been highly comical if it wasn't so heartbreaking.

The next day Grandma Ruby told me I should have taken some of her eggs away first, but by then it was too late. There was no way I'd try again and risk getting one of the chicks killed. I'd already decided to raise them myself, and she could hatch hers if she had any, and we'd deal with it that way. After a few more days, I felt certain it wasn't going to happen with the hen. After telling Ruby I thought it best to bring her back, that I was pretty sure the eggs were not going to hatch, she agreed and asked me to first put them into a pan full of water to make sure. If they floated, there were no chicks. They all floated.

With a heavy heart, I returned the hen to Ruby. She had wanted me to keep her, as a gift, as a sort of living bond between the two of us in our mutual hobby. She wanted to share with us the sight of a mother hen being trailed by a group of rowdy little peepers. "I don't know why I like chickens so much," she'd declared on several occasions. Once she confided that her husband, who passed away seventeen years earlier, didn't share her fondness and never wanted her to raise chickens. "After he died," she said, a determined expression settling over her beautifully wizened face, "one of the first things I did was buy some chickens."

The girls named the chicks within the first hour of their arrival. The Sebrights became Jessica and Suzie, the Silkies Jane and Zelda, the little black one Julianna, and the yellow chick, Kayley. "Great names for roosters," I said. We wouldn't know their actual gender for about six weeks, when the males were supposed to begin their first attempts at cock-a-doodle-doo-ing.

I admit that at first I was just a teensy bit anxious taking care of the babies. The temperature in the box had to be regulated to around 95 degrees the first week and reduced about five degrees weekly for about a month until they feathered out. I monitored the temperature daily and fussed with the position of the light each time I entered the room, which was often. Twice each night, I checked on them before I went to bed. I worried whether they'd have retina damage due to the constant illumination. Through my research on baby chick diseases I learned about something called "pasting up" — a condition in which runny droppings get stuck to their bottoms, causing elimination problems. So, with a bit of tissue, I pulled dried baby chick poop off their butts. *I can't believe I'm wiping chicken's asses!* I thought. I'd metamorphosed into their mother.

Peeking into the room during the day, I continually spied Lily with little black Julianna in her small, chubby hands. "Put that chick down and go wash your hands!" I said over and over. They had a lot of leeway to play with them, but with no admonishments, they would undoubtedly try to take them into the bath with them. I'd already caught them putting chicks in dollhouse cars (they said the chicks looked out the windows), on the dollhouse motorcycle, and on top of the dollhouse itself. They asked if they could take them out to the swing set. My biggest fear was that one of the chicks would accidentally be killed, ruining the whole experience and no doubt creating fodder for adult therapy sessions.

Soon Zora and I began digging worms for their breakfast. We all gathered around the box and one of us would dangle a wiggler until a chick grabbed it. The chick would then run around the box with the others peeping in hot pursuit. Zora gave them voices. "No, Julianna, you can't have it," she'd have Suzie say. "It's my worm. It's mine! It's mine!" The girls laughed and squealed as the chicks raced round and round. Zora yelled when her favorite chick got a worm and the others tried to take it away. "Stay away! It's Kayley's! No!" She'd block the others off with her hands, and I'd say, "Don't!" We'd all gross out when one would have a long worm almost swallowed and another would pull on what was still hanging out of its mouth.

We discovered we could buy live crickets at the pet store. We'd buy a dozen or two at a time and dump the contents of the plastic bags into the box. The chicks would be on them with lightning speed. I recalled reading somewhere that the skeletal structure of chickens was very much like some of the meat-eating dinosaurs, and it wasn't hard to imagine little Velociraptors lurking under the fluff. The girls and I, accused by Andy of being bloodthirsty in our enthusiasm, knew we were just doing what any good mother hens would do.

\* \* \*

The chicks grew rapidly. Like Grandma Ruby said, it was almost like watching popcorn. Halfway through their third week, the Sebrights sported fully feathered wings. Kayley had a tiny comb and a few snow-white wing and leg feathers, Julianna had black tail feathers, distinct but tiny, sticking straight up, and the Silkies' down was even fluffier, especially on their large blackish-grey feet. When I found one of the Sebrights perched up on top of the box one morning, I knew it was time to take them to their outdoor home.

At first, I kept a light on near one corner of the chicken shack because summer nights can be chilly in Colorado and the chicks weren't totally feathered out. As in their box indoors, they piled up to sleep, snuggling under the light. Within a couple of days, however, Julianna and one of the Sebrights started to roost away from the crowd. Then one night, after a couple of weeks, I turned the light off. The terrified peeping that ensued alarmed me. I realized how tenaciously they clung to the warmth- and light-giving bulb. They would have to be weaned from Mother Illumination. I first lowered the wattage to 40 for a few days, then I made a trip to the grocery store and spent over three dollars on a 12-watt nightlight bulb for chickens who were afraid of the dark.

They were spoiled in so many ways. We brought them table scraps and other treats on a daily basis and found out their absolute favorite (non-living) foods were corn on the cob, cantaloupe, and homemade split pea soup. They grabbed bits of ham from the soup and ran around covetously like they had with the crickets and worms. The girls and I began catching grasshoppers for the chicks and discovered there were five different species living in our backyard. I showed them how to distinguish grasshoppers in the nymph and adult (with wings) stages.

We checked out books on chickens and found out our Sebrights were not Golden, but Silver. According to the illustration, almost every feather on their bodies, wings, and tails would become a bright white, edged completely around in gloss black. Instead of the rounded bodies of most poultry breeds, their body shapes, as they matured, would become more tapered, like other birds. The homeliest of the chicks, they began to develop their slight builds and distinctly patterned feathering, taking on an elegant, even aristocratic, appearance. We learned they belonged to a breed developed over a 30-year period by Sir John Sebright of England in the early 1800s. The birds were remarkable in the poultry world for the fact that the male and female had the same feathering, shape, and coloring. However, we soon noticed that one of them was definitely growing a more pronounced comb and wattles — we had one of each sex.

Right from the beginning with the Silkies, Jane (my personal darling) was bigger than Zelda. But it was three months before there was enough distinction in his wattles and comb to declare Jane a John since Silkies also have near-identical plumage. The breed is prized for its gentleness and broodiness, and the hens are often used commercially to hatch eggs, especially pheasant eggs. In my reading I learned that broodiness, the desire to set on a clutch of eggs, to become a mother, had almost been bred out of many modern breeds of fowl.

Lily's Julianna, with "her" tail feathers growing more pronounced every day (Grandma Ruby's own foolproof way of determining a male), was also a he. Julianna was a Black Rosecomb, a breed named for their unique combs. It lies low on their heads, is square in front, terminates to a pointed spike at the back, and is covered with small bumps. Julianna's comb and wattles were vivid red, and he sported white disk-shaped ear-lobes, part of the rooster's "dangly parts," as I called them, below the ear holes. His earlobes were perfectly round, enamel white, and added a jaunty, pirate-like air to his already cocky countenance. With lustrous green-black feathers, including long, arching tail feathers, he was handsome, and he knew it. He was the first to crow. Lily renamed him Garrett.

Zora's bird also turned out to be a cockerel, though she remained in denial for a long time. As snow-white feathers on his rounded body and large orange feet began to replace the down, we soon ID'd him as a Cochin, of the bantam variety once known as Pekin. We read that Cochin chickens, originating from China, were the cause of an episode of "poultry-mania" in England in 1845. When they were presented as gifts to Queen Victoria, the public was quite taken with the breed's beauty, size, and gentle nature. Nearly overnight, Victorian yuppies began longing to own one, and before the mania died down, some paid more than an average worker's yearly pay for a single "Shanghai Fowl." Kayley, like the description predicted, was sweet-tempered and could be scooped up without fuss by simply bending over and sliding a hand or two under his soft breast. When he began to crow, his voice was deep and unobtrusive but also somewhat fit the (exaggerated) description of Queen Victoria's birds who were said to "roar like lions."

So, we ended up with only two hens and four cocks. Although their crowing was not yet a problem, we knew we probably wouldn't be able to keep the males, though I told the girls we would for as long as possible. As the days passed, I began to hope that maybe we would be able to keep them until next spring and try for chicks again — Sebrights and Silkies, and maybe a few hybrids. I was amazed to find out that most of our neighbors had been totally oblivious to the "Morn of Grandma Ruby's Rooster." I let them know what we were up to and asked them to tell me if the roosters became a nuisance.

\* \* \*

For about six weeks, we basked in perfect poultry happiness. Then one morning when I went to feed them, I found a cat crouched on one of the fence posts of the chicken yard. The birds were huddled in a corner, terrified. I shooed the cat and counted the chickens; one was missing. My heart raced as I frantically searched the backyard. Nothing. I searched the alley, thinking that perhaps the cat took the chicken over the fence via the tree next to the coop. Still nothing.

Zora came out, and I calmly told her what happened, and that the female Sebright was gone. We looked some more and as I neared the girls' inflatable three-foot-deep swimming pool I spotted her floating, wings spread wide, eyes closed, her graceful neck resting motionless on top of the water. In a low voice I said, "Oh, Zora. I found her." Zora came over, and we stood there, looking, fighting back tears. I went into the house to find something to pick her up with, and Lily followed me out. It then occurred to me there was no reason I should be squeamish to touch her — I *knew* her. I lifted her out and placed her tenderly on the paper towel. The girls petted her. There were no signs of injury. Apparently, the cat had frightened her into flying over the four-foot fence and into the pool.

We buried the Sebright near the girls' "castle," a semi-circle of small Siberian elms. I gathered smooth, pretty rocks to cover the grave, and Zora found a red and white plastic Fisher Price chicken to perch on top. After a few minutes, she added part of a small, spherical, broken crystal prism from our kitchen-windowsill collection of odds and ends.

"I got this because Jessica liked shiny things," she explained. We gathered around the grave on our knees, and I said a few words about Jessica's sweetness and goodness, how we all loved her and would miss her very much. Privately, I also felt disappointment at losing our male Sebright's mate and fully half our hen population. There would be no Sebright chicks next spring.

It never occurred to me that the pool was a danger. Grandma Ruby cautioned me about the four-foot fence around the coop. "Oh, they'll be able to get over that pretty soon," she said on her first visit, but I hadn't been very concerned. We had a six-foot fence around the yard and we secured the chickens in their coop each night. Besides, Grandma Ruby's chickens ranged her yard freely among her young cat Tweety, two miniature poodles, and various neighborhood felines (her ninety-some-year-old neighbor next door had *thirteen*). The only problems she'd had came from a marauding raccoon that killed a rooster the year before, and the time, years earlier, when some obviously psychotic teenage boys abducted and murdered another.

We had our own pet carnivores, but I'd never seen our cat, Merlin, a 17-year-old bag o' bones Siamese, hunt for anything other than a good place to nap. He showed absolutely no recognition that a flock of chickens had invaded his turf. Our 14-year-old black Labrador retriever, Cato, was not only a creampuff, but he'd been blind in one eye since age two when he was kicked by a horse and was now nearly blind in the other from a cataract. He sometimes stood at the chicken fence, on now-unsteady legs, and barked a few times, tail wagging. I imagined he saw blurs of chickens and surely smelled them and was making the canine assertion that he had some authority around here yet. Our only potential problem was Alice, the 18-month-old Dalmatian we adopted the summer before. A spotted hell-on-four-paws (and my outlaw shrub-pruner the winter before), she was nonetheless our darling. Alice had menaced an injured wild bird early that spring, but only by bouncing around and barking; she never tried to hurt it. Knowing her potential for frolicking destruction, however, I kept close tabs on her.

When Andy came home from work, I told him about the ordeal we'd been through and that we *had* to build a covered run the next day, on Saturday. After a morning of almost non-stop nagging on my part, we started the project. It took us only about three hours of constant bickering to put it together. I mixed the concrete for the fence posts and stapled the chicken wire, while Andy cut and assembled the posts and rails.

Alice dug under the run the very next Saturday. The chickens escaped, and again I ran around, heart racing, hunting and gathering. This time I found only three. Zelda (the female Silkie), and the other Sebright were missing. Finding evidence of Alice's digging at the wire fence surrounding the vegetable garden, right next to the chicken shack, I investigated there. Sitting very still in a patch of grass was the Sebright. I took him into the house and examined him, discovering some minor scratches under a wing and a scrape on his lower right leg. He had apparently injured himself trying to escape Alice by squeezing under a low spot in the fence. Vehicle-less (my car was undergoing repair at the time) I phoned our veterinarian. Dr. Westrich told me that if I couldn't get in, I should clean the wounds with hydrogen peroxide, keep the bird in a quiet place, and watch him. He also said that if the other one hadn't been found yet, it probably meant that she wouldn't be found alive.

I set up a box for Suzie the male Sebright in the girls' playroom and went to search for Zelda again. I found her immediately — alive and well! She had been hiding out on the other side of the enclosed run — between it and a bale of straw. When I spotted her, she was venturing out into the open, peeping frantically to her coop-mates on the other side. Quietly I thanked whoever was in charge of her safety for having mercy on me as well.

Early the next morning I found the Sebright hopping around his box. I picked him up for a minute and murmured consolingly to him, and when I left, he made loud, distressed peeps. I comforted him again, and again he cried out when I left. The third time I went in, he was perched on top of the box on his good leg. *Maybe he'll be okay outside with his buddies,* I thought, as it was apparent he would be miserable inside alone. In the chicken shack, his brothers and sister, noisy and excited, gathered around him, but he was hopping around so pitifully I changed my mind about leaving him. He needed rest.

As I walked away from the other chickens with Suzie pressed against my breast, he began to protest — loudly and incessantly. With a nagging conscience, I returned him to his flock.

The next couple of days he seemed to be okay except for his leg, which I could tell was causing him pain. As the other chickens filed out of the coop into the garden to scratch for bugs and eat young weeds he, protested loudly, then reluctantly hopped along behind them. Otherwise he ate, drank, and rested normally. I checked twice daily for signs of infection and found none.

On the third day I noticed the bottom of his injured leg was swollen, so I called Dr. Westrich. Though he didn't treat birds, he agreed to check him out that afternoon. I figured the bird's leg was infected and that it would need to be drained, then the doctor would put him on antibiotics. I wasn't really worried and thought it would be an educational experience for the girls.

A friend of the girls', Christiana, was spending the day with us, and her mother said she could come along. As I carried the basket holding Suzie into the veterinarian's office, three little girls dressed up in tea party clothes — long colorful dresses, shawls, rhinestone jewelry, and parasols — traipsed behind me. In the examining room, we gathered around Dr. Westrich as he gently lifted the bird from the basket, speaking to him softly and reassuringly.

He examined him for only a few moments before pointing out the area above the swelling. "Do you see here, where the leg bends?" he said. "If you compare it with the other leg, you can see it shouldn't do that. It's broken."

My heart sank.

"And his foot doesn't have the healthy pink color that the other has. That shows that the area is not getting circulation."

"So it's getting *gangrene*?" I asked, completely horrified.

"It looks like that's probably what's happening."

I asked if it could be amputated, and he said he thought it could. He told me he thought the chicken would eventually be able to get around like other animal amputees, but that he didn't do surgery on birds. He said he'd call a doctor he knew, see what he thought, and try to set up an appointment.

The children had been silently taking in the unfolding drama. Zora now spoke. "Do we have to watch the other doctor do that?"

"God no!" I blurted.

The doctor, a father of six grown children of his own, smiled at me sympathetically.

We waited at the front desk. After a few minutes, Dr. Westrich came back out and carefully explained, "I spoke with Dr. Abernathy. He said that in the case of amputations, the birds eventually develop a disease, an arthritic condition in the other leg, that ultimately debilitates them."

"So there's nothing that can be done?" I asked tearfully.

"You could go ahead with the amputation," he said, "but I wouldn't recommend it."

"We'd be putting off the inevitable. . . ." I paused, trying to find an escape route from reality. "Are you sure it would be the same for him," I asked, "since he's a miniature chicken? They only weigh about a fourth as much as a regular-sized bird."

"I'm afraid so."

"I can't imagine putting him through more than I already have."

"We can euthanize him here," the doctor offered.

The next words did not come easily. "I think that would probably be best." I looked over at the girls chatting happily near the waiting room's aquarium. I felt dread, devastation and a large measure of self-loathing.

"You can use the examining room to talk to them," Dr. Westrich said quietly.

Trying hard to hold on to what little composure I felt I had left, I called the girls back into the examining room. Crouched before them, tears brimming, I told them what had to be done.

Zora, in a consoling tone I'd never heard her use before said, "Okay, Mom."

Lily's eyes filled with tears for a few moments before asking, "Are we going to bury him next to Jessica?"

It felt like I was co-starring in the absolute worst, most melodramatic soap opera of all time — and the scene had to play out. We went to say our goodbyes to Suzie. Before taking him away, the doctor asked if we wanted the body to take home, or if they should dispose of it.

"Please do it here," I said. I knew I was copping out. The girls could probably handle it, but I could not. Not two pet burials in as many weeks, even if they were "just" chickens.

The doctor brought back the basket and left the room to begin the euthanasia. Taking out my checkbook and pen, I asked the receptionist how much the bill came to.

"The doctor says there's no charge."

"You can't be serious. I *have* to pay you."

"He said not to charge you." She smiled. "So don't worry about it."

Back home, I found I had to make a decision. On one hand, I could not bear any more tragedies. If anything else happened, the chicken experiment was officially over. And I meant it. We were down to four chickens, three of them male, and I wasn't sure how long we'd be keeping them. After a summer of work and dreams, we had one hen. On the other hand, we'd gone this far — we'd built the covered run, and I'd laid cement blocks around the parameter so the damn dog (I'd cursed her bitterly when we returned home that day) couldn't dig under it. I had nearly 25 pounds of feed, plus all the poultry paraphernalia — waterers, feeders, vitamins, and a wire cage. The girls had bonded with their favorites, who luckily were still alive, and we'd taken a lot of pictures, documenting our "fun," including some wonderful ones of the girls holding the birds while wearing their tea-party clothes. I decided I'd give it one more try. But to make it worthwhile, I needed to find a few replacement hens.

I browsed the local paper's Classifieds under "Farm Animals" and found no chickens for sale. Not profitable enough in the big city, I deduced. The County Fair had come and gone, and the only other places I knew of to buy poultry this time of year were the weekly livestock auction in the rural town of Calhan and the State Fair, now going on in the nearby city of Pueblo. Still quite the livestock novice, I was more than a little wary of buying at auction, so I called the Fair. A helpful woman informed me they'd be selling chickens from the Junior Division Livestock Show in a couple of weeks.

On Friday of Labor Day weekend, we set out at 9:00 A.M. The trunk contained our outfitting: a wood-sided red wagon, two cages, and a basket, all made comfy with soft straw bedding. I had recovered from the previous tragedies and was looking forward to our hen quest, hoping to find my own objet d'desire, a mille fleur booted bantam that I'd seen in the chicken books. "Mille fleur" is French for thousand flowers, and "booted" refers to this breed's feathered legs. It's a fancy tan, black, and white bird, with feathers that are spangled, mottled, or stippled in pattern — sometimes all three. Some of the tail feathers are two-toned — tan on one side and black on the other, and most have white tips. Lily says they look like they have white polka dots. She decided she wanted to find a black chicken, to pair with Garrett, and Zora hoped to find either another Cochin or an Araucana.

At the fair, we found a parking spot near the entrance. The morning air was refreshing and the grounds quiet. Andy came along but couldn't stay long because he had to return to work. After taking Zora and Lily on a quick run through the Arts and Crafts Building while Andy browsed the new trucks, we headed for the Small Livestock Building. We made a bee-line for the chickens, passing areas filled with pigeons, ducks, geese, turkeys, and rabbits. The sale had begun at 8:00 A.M., and over a fourth of the cages were empty; with buyers milling about, the pressure was on.

Searching through cages of bantams, we found no Cochins or Araucanas, but I located a half dozen mille fleurs, and my decision was made. Lily fell in love with a black hen who wasn't for sale. Her second choice was a little Rhode Island red. The hen seemed gentle and was handsome — her dark reddish-brown body embellished with black, lacy-topped tail feathers. An American girl, something new for our collection. I heartily approved. The Polish breed chickens, referred to as such even though they are thought to have originated in Belgium, caught my eye. They're the type with the big feathery topknots that resemble haute couture hats from the 1950s. I call them Dr. Seuss birds. Zora couldn't be persuaded into getting one; she declared them ugly.

She took her time selecting her perfect pullet, a medium-sized mixed breed. The young female was admittedly beautiful, with a body that was graceful and tapered, like the Sebrights', but she was an Amazon. Her long neck displayed a multitude of thin, white, vertical feathers, setting off a body tastefully speckled in black and white. Her wing feathers were tipped white, and her tail feathers black — the latter sticking up at a haughty angle. She had long, slate-blue legs, sharp golden-brown eyes, and a small red comb and wattles. After being around them a while, one can sense a bird's personality. Lily's Rhode Island red and my mille fleur were easy to read — mellow. This bird was different. I detected an attitude of arrogance.

"Are you sure?" I asked Zora. "Why don't we look around one more time?"

"I want this one," she said.

I looked at the price on the cage. Twenty-five dollars. The hen I'd picked out was ten, and Lily's was only six. But I knew there was no use trying to persuade Zora otherwise; she was a girl who knew what she wanted. Always had been. From birth.

As we were paying for the birds, a photographer from the *Pueblo Chieftain* came up and asked if he could take a few pictures. Enthusiastic, but wary of having Zora and Lily both hold birds they were unfamiliar with at the same time, I asked that he photograph Zora first. She happened to be wearing an ensemble — a black and white patterned dress with a white collar and matching beret, both embellished with small, red cloth roses — that perfectly matched her new chicken. Then he photographed Lily, whose hair needed brushing (though I didn't notice it at the time), and whose dark

51

brown, blue, and black-checked dress probably made the Rhode Island Red nearly disappear on film.

As a final shot, he posed them together. Then Zora's bird got away and had to be chased down the long aisle of caged birds by a man with a net. While this took place, Andy returned. He'd been gone most of the time, visiting the hot tub display.

"What's going on?" he asked, eyeing the photographer.

"Oh, nothing. Just memorializing the occasion," I replied, feeling a bit bitchy. "This photographer asked if he could take pictures for the newspaper."

"Pictures for the paper?"

"Yeah, and you missed it."

Andy didn't respond to that remark, trying, as usual (well, more than I did), to keep it cool-headed when it came to bickering around the girls.

We loaded the chickens into the cages and basket, then into our little red wagon. In the car, the girls each happily held a caged bird, and I kept my chicken-in-a-basket with me in the front seat. It crossed my mind it would be very weird indeed if we got into an accident with three chickens riding with us inside the car. The girls chattered in the back, picking out names for their new pets and talking about being in the newspaper. Lily exclaimed, "Now we're going to be famous. We won't have to go to school anymore!" We all laughed, but I had a sinking feeling. Knowledgeable about photography, I felt almost certain they would use Zora's picture. Either way, one of them would be disappointed, unless they used the picture of them together, which I thought unlikely. I tried to broach the subject, but the girls were too jolly to consider anything negative.

Zora named her hen Aphrodite, after the Greek goddess of love and beauty. Lily's favorite goddess was Athena, the goddess of war and wisdom, so that became the Rhode Island red's name, and they christened mine Hera, queen of the gods (we'd been reading Greek mythology that summer). I loved their choices. One urban chicken farmer I knew of had named all her hens after country and western stars — Reba, Dolly, and so on, so I was pleased that the girls had picked up a theme of their own, without my help.

Since the chickens were all females, introducing them to the flock went off without a hitch. That night at dusk I slipped them through the door and after a few clucks and rustlings everything went quiet.

The next day they began to get to know one another and re-establish the pecking order. I wasn't sure who was at the very top — it was either Zora's Kayley or Lily's Garrett — but Aphrodite began to assert her dominance right away. Towering over them all, she stretched her neck high and challenged one and all to question her authority. Zora and Lily screamed as she pecked at each and every one of the other chickens, including the males, when they were so insolent as to not bow down to her majesty. After a few kicks and pecks sent back her way, however, she soon realized that the boys were supposed to be the bosses in the chicken world, and she began to take on a more ladylike demeanor. And I stopped calling her Mighty Aphrodite, which had irritated Zora. My bird, meek Hera, queen of all the gods and goddesses, immediately sunk to the absolute bottom of the order, and in her position stayed several feet away from the other chickens most of the time. She was the last to approach the daily pan of table scraps. Gentle and wise Athena took a middle rank.

The day after we brought them home, in late afternoon, Zora and Lily came running into the house. "We found an egg! We found an egg!" they yelled, holding the small, light brown gift from Athena. It was absolute magic to them, as if they'd discovered a jewel in the nesting box straw. I felt proud too — our very first egg.

I called the paper and found out that it was indeed Zora's picture they used in the Saturday edition. Lily was upset when I broke the news, but not as upset as when we finally got our copies of the paper in the mail the next week. There, on page 5A, we saw a full-color, six-by-nine-inch picture of Zora holding Aphrodite. An accompanying article flashed the headline: "Lots of Cool Chicks at the Fair." Lily took one look and ran out of the house. We could hear her through the opened back door, at the swing set, crying as if her heart would break. Taking only a few seconds to marvel at the picture (we were expecting a small black and white), and how fun it all *almost* was, I went to try to comfort Lily.

She was swinging and crying so hard her face was blotched red and white. "Why did they use Zora's and not mine? Everybody thinks Zora is better than me."

"That's not true, Lily. Her chicken just happened to show up better against her clothes. I'm sure that's why they used it. Please don't cry, honey."

I told her that no one in this whole city of Colorado Springs would even see the picture because you can't even buy a paper from Pueblo here. I told her that no one we knew would even know Zora was in the paper unless we showed them. I told her about other members of the family who'd been in the paper or on television for fun things and that her turn would surely come soon too. Of course, nothing I said was good enough to soothe her; yet another lesson in motherhood. It was unexpected that Lily, who had always been very easy-going, would be so envious, so traumatized

I wondered if a summer of backyard chicken raising, all these ups and downs, had been worth the roller coaster ride after all.

My answer came several weeks later when Lily's preschool teacher asked if I could bring the banties in for "Sharing Time." I decided to bring the three gentlest birds, Kayley, Jane, and, of course, our egg-layer, Athena.

I prepared for the talk by gathering some feathers, boiling a few eggs, store-bought large and bantam for size comparison, and hauling out our globe so I could show the children where all chickens originated, the island of Java. As I lugged in the wooden cage holding Kayley and Athena, Lily looked up at me with sparkling eyes. The teacher told me I had five minutes. First, I presented Jane, the Silkie, who was in a separate basket. I talked about his unique feathers and where his breed was from (the same place the Disney character Mulan was from!). I passed around feathers and eggs. Then, as I went to get Kayley, I asked Lily if she'd help with Athena.

She deftly gathered up her little hen and was immediately surrounded by classmates who wanted to pet and hold her. It was Lily's turn in the spotlight.

In the car, she told me how she had felt at show and tell. "Mom," she said, "I learned something today."

I looked in the rear-view mirror. "What's that, sweetie?"

"That happiness can make tears come to your eyes."

"What?" I asked.

"I was so happy when I saw Athena I felt like crying — and then I couldn't stop smiling."

* * *

It had been one intense summer. If someone had told me what was going to happen in our little experiment — the profound highs and lows, the multitude of things to learn, to question, and to feel, over something so seemingly, inanely, simple — I wouldn't have believed it. Like an egg incubating under the warm down of its mother's bosom, the process of learning, of experiencing, took its own sweet time. I ended up reviewing a simple lesson: the most rewarding experiences in life are never, ever easy. And one more. That if you are ever adventurous enough to find yourself doing something a little deviant, a little unexpected — say raising chickens in the city — you just might find you end up with something to crow about.

# The Ellie Mae Gene

Lily's kindergarten teacher waved me over as I arrived to pick up my girl after school. "I just had a call from a friend at a pet store," said the grey-haired Mrs. Miller, holding the door open as children bounded past her to freedom. "Someone dropped off a pair of sugar gliders today, and they need a home, *fast*. Are you interested?"

"What are sugar gliders?" I felt a little stupid that I had to ask.

"They're real cute. Miniature flying squirrels. Marsupials."

*Marsupials.* . . . My mind caressed the word, and an exciting picture began to form: little mammals with *pouches, flying around in a large cage.* I imagined them in our living room, entertaining us with their acrobatics. It would be circus-like, the daring young marsupials on the flying trapeze!

Lily stood by my side as her classmates ran to their moms and dads and the teacher waited patiently for my reply. Mrs. Miller was an animal lover, and she knew I was too. She had bunnies, bantam chickens, a goose with a bum wing, and a classroom tarantula. She was also a black belt in karate. In other words, this woman was fearless, the perfect educator for five and six year olds.

"Well?" she said.

At that moment, another mom came up and asked Mrs. Miller if she could get a permission slip for an upcoming field trip. Mrs. Miller said sure and indicated to me to wait a moment while she ran back to her classroom.

I started thinking it over. You'd better believe I wanted to say YES to the marsupials.

I blame the Ellie Mae gene. . . .

* * *

The Ellie gene means one thing: a passion for animals. My childhood was filled with a fascination for them. As I toddler I chased lizards around on our patio in California; when I was three we went to Sea World, and I clapped my hands together during the dolphin show, crying, "Flipper! Flipper!" (I thought I had recognized a TV star.) But with six kids between two marriages, my parents/step-parents weren't interested in adding pets to their lists of responsibilities. Still, I managed, a few times, to bring one home temporarily, but it never lasted.

Instead of the real thing, I fed my animal mania through books. My favorites were *Curious George, Pippi Longstocking, Charlotte's Web,* and anything by Dr. Seuss. The perfect life seemed to include a monkey on one's shoulder, a horse you could have in the house, or at the minimum, interaction with a smart-ass cat who wore a hat. As I grew older, I discovered more realistic books like *My Side of the Mountain,* about a boy, Sam Gribbley, who runs off into the woods and lives on his own by hunting and gathering. Sam awed me with his knowledge of wild plants, and I thrilled at the peregrine falcon he raised as a companion and hunting partner. For months I daydreamed about living wild and free like Sam did.

Then there were the TV programs. I admired Ellie Mae Clampett of *The Beverly Hillbillies.* Ellie Mae was unrefined, but, to me, hers was a womanhood to aspire to. She was unselfconscious, pure of heart, physically strong, fearless, gorgeous, and, most importantly, devoted to her "critters." And what critters they were! Ellie swam with seals in the "cement pond," brought raccoons into the mansion, and even rode around in her family's big white convertible with a tiger. To me, it looked like bliss.

A little later, as I learned about the real-life adventures of Jane Goodall and her chimpanzees and Jacques Cousteau's famous oceanic explorations on the *Calypso,* reality completely eclipsed the kid stuff. The first career I dreamed about was oceanographer.

This shift coincided with my sexual awakening. At age 13 I walked to the grocery store and bought my first grown-up paperback novel, Peter Benchley's *Jaws.* I read the novel in a single eye-opening summer afternoon, skimming through the shark biology and lingering over the adulterous affair between Ellen Brody and

Hooper. The Ellie Mae gene went into retreat as my passion for another "species," *homo sapiens masculum*, as my sister Karen called them, blossomed.

Just four years later would I meet the counterpoint to my animal love, the yang to my yin. I was 17; three siblings and I were now living with our mother in Colorado. The first time I laid eyes on Andy, it was instant animal magnetism. He was beautiful — muscular, blue-eyed, square-jawed, a few years older than I, and he made me laugh by doing things like singing Pat Benatar's *Heartbreaker* to me in front of our friends on our first date. What started out as lust and enchantment grew to love. I discovered that, like me, Andy came from a dysfunctional family, with their own troubles and secrets, but his family was made up of seven siblings and parents who had stayed married. And while outwardly conservative, the family had a delicious hedonistic bent — a trait that extended to animal ownership.

The first time I visited Andy's family, two golden retrievers and a black, scruffy, three-legged terrier came bounding toward us, barking like crazy.

"The fat one's Jesse," said Andy, pointing to one of the retrievers. Jesse said hello by dropping a drool-covered ball on my sneaker. I petted him and remarked on his soft strawberry-blond fur. "And that's Roscoe," Andy said, pointing at the other retriever. Roscoe barked once more, then came up and stuck his nose right in my crotch, his way of saying howdy.

I pushed Roscoe's head away and pointed to the scraggly black terrier with three legs who was still barking and keeping his distance. "Who's that?"

"That's Coty. We call him 'The Fly.'"

"How mean!" (Still, I laughed.)

In the kitchen, I met the elderly collie, Rocky, who was lying on a braided rug. Andy said he was once the fiercest. Rocky looked up briefly before nodding back off to sleep. Sitting at the kitchen table, I witnessed a feline ball of fur, Gigi, leave a kitchen cabinet. It wasn't long before I met housecats Mouse and Buck as well. The smells, the chaos, the copious hair that filled that house was surprising, and, I thought, rather wonderful. And outside, in the backyard of the one-acre property, was a real live horse!

It was all so attractive, so wild, and energetic. At my mother's suburban house everything was neat inside, with neighborhood covenants to make damn sure the outside conformed to exacting standards as well. House colors had to be approved, RVs weren't allowed on the streets, clotheslines were taboo, and there was even a "no pup tent" rule for kids who wanted to have fun with some backyard camping. I disliked Stepford, even though we had a dog there, Topo, my mom's small Pekingese/poodle mix, what she called a "peekapoo." An ongoing problem was when Topo would leave a poopoo on the white carpet when everyone was at work and school. At Andy's house, poo was no big deal. Not much was, and that seemed, at least in those early years, to be a great *liberation*.

* * *

By this time Lily had told Malcolm, the little boy whose mother had gone inside the school with Mrs. Miller, that we might get "flying squirrels," and the two of them were pretending to be flying squirrels, running around, leaping, spreading their arms out.

"I'm getting some frogs for my birthday!" said Malcolm.

Lily looked envious.

* * *

I recalled all those years ago when Andy and I started dating; he could tell that animals set my heart aflutter, and he wooed me with pets. A former aquarium hobbyist, he gifted me with a 10-gallon tank for my bedroom, his first love token. The fish we picked out included a pair of golden kissing fish, *gouramis*. A few months later he bought me a pair of parakeets that I named Jake and Pearl. Andy and I became like the fish and the fowl, inseparable.

The night I believe I truly fell in love with Andy was a night like most school nights. We'd been hanging out, watching TV downstairs in his basement bedroom, when he left to make us a snack. It took forever for him to return, and when he walked in the door he was crying. I'd never seen him show that kind of emotion before.

I jumped up. "What happened?"

"I stepped on that kitten," he told me, wiping his eyes. "He was on the stairs." The kitten, a grey-striped cutie from Gigi's most recent litter, had taken up with Andy during the last two weeks, following him around when he got home from work, jumping out at him in invitations to play, meowing to be picked up. They played and cuddled every day. That night, the kitten had been asleep on the dark stairs.

I was witnessing a devastation I didn't know quite how to react to. This was my man, who had a construction job, worked on cars, and had been in a few fistfights — in *grief*. Tenderness overwhelmed me. It wasn't long after that we got our own kitten, and after I graduated from high school, a place of our own. We'd been together in animal bliss ever since.

With parenthood the pets had increased, and I had been getting my Ellie Mae on. We were all having fun but . . . flying squirrels?

\* \* \*

Mrs. Miller was back, and she was staring at me, waiting patiently for an answer. I had to decide, did I want to add marsupials to our menagerie?

I snapped out of my reverie and faced the facts. In the past month our family had acquired its largest ever new pet bonanza — two cast-off Easter ducklings *and* a lop-eared bunny, who still needed a hutch. The rabbit was largely the result of Mrs. Miller's influence; she'd shared her collection of rabbits with her students, prompting Lily to beg for one until we gave in. These animals, in addition to our collection of six chickens, two dogs, a canary, and tropical fish . . . there was *absolutely no way*.

"Um, I'd better not. . . ." I said, visions of sugar gliders still dancing, but not with much vigor, in my head. "I'd like to, but I've already got my hands full with the zoo back home."

"Okay," she said, and left it at that.

Like a rabbit, or a deer, I gathered Lily and hightailed it out of there before I changed my mind.

Afterwards, I realized with growing horror that for a few enchanted minutes I had actually, seriously, considered saying *yes* — to a cage of flying squirrels! On this day I began to seriously scrutinize my fascination with the four-legged ones, the winged and finned ones, my animal loves. Why this nearly irresistible attraction? It didn't matter if it walked, crawled, flew, swam, or skittered — if it was a critter — I was into it. Where did this come from? Why me?

I can only offer as an explanation — the Ellie Mae gene.

# Fish Styx

At last, break time. I plopped, sweaty and tired, into my favorite chair, a magazine in one hand and a glass of iced tea in the other. It'd been a non-stop summer day — kids home, chores inside and out, and it was Andy's 40th birthday. I'd weeded the garden, tidied the house, baked a cake, pumped the old water from the girls' three-foot-deep pool into the flower beds, and scrubbed down the pools' sides. It was time to relax. I put my feet up, took a sip of tea. *Ahhhhhh.*

I was in the middle of an interesting article when six-year-old Lily slammed the back door, ran through the kitchen, and stopped directly in front of my chair. What I noticed first were her eyes — they were wide in alarm.

Paradoxically, her voice came out calm, matter-of-fact. "Well," she said, "I guess we'll just have to get more goldfish."

*Oh my God!* I bolted from the chair. I knew exactly what had happened. After I took the pump out of the swimming pool, I put it back into the fish pond. I'd unplugged a cord, but not the right one. I'd drained the fish pond! I tore outside and screeched to a halt. The ghastly spectacle of fifteen flopping fish in a gallon-sized mudhole greeted my own wide eyes. *What should I do?* My thoughts were frantic. *Grab the hose? Or grab a bucket and run for the water-filled bathtub pond close by? Or maybe the newly-filled swimming pool?* I wanted to do all three, at once. For a painfully comic second, I stood there frozen.

I raced for the hose. The goldfish seemed okay, but the two costly koi had x's in their eyes. As I fished them out, I bitterly remembered how I'd admired them just days before, marveled at how big and beautiful they'd grown over the last year, since the day we brought them home as small fry with tiny Fu Manchu mustaches. I also recalled, bitterly, what I'd recently read about these ornamental carp. A book on water gardening described how the Japanese take special care of their koi, believing they contain the souls of their ancestors.

In Japan, many koi have lived over a century. I'd killed ours off within a year, and on Andy's birthday. Oh, the dark karma!

As the pond filled, I thought back to our other goldfish dramas. The first one, a lighter tale, had occurred four years earlier in our first water garden. The sunken and rusty clawfoot tub held a pot of horsetail and some water hyacinths, along with a few pet store goldfish, rare bargains at 25 cents each. Zora and Lily, tiny tots then at ages five and two, enjoyed picking them out from the big tank of feeder fish.

"I want the one with the orange heart on its head," Zora said, pointing to the single orange-heart-headed white goldfish among the cast of hundreds. The pet shop girl, a dazzling fish-netter, snared the little guy after a short but harrowing chase, then remarked that she'd never seen one quite like him before.

Lily said, "I want Whitey," as she pointed to an albino one.

"We're saving their lives, you know," I told our girls. "If no one buys them, they'll end up as snake, or maybe even piranha, food." I enjoyed letting them know that we were not merely goldfish customers, but liberators of death-row feeder fish. It was a special mommy thing I liked to do — making our outings both as educational and as dramatic as possible.

"Or sometimes they're turtle food," added the girl with the net, who was now transferring Whitey into a plastic bag.

We bought six. The girls had a jolly time on the way home, fighting over whose turn it was to hold the bag o' fish.

The thrill of creating our own pond, a miniature ecosystem that thrived and bloomed and held watery life exceeded my expectations. I decided to overwinter the fish inside, in an aquarium, and I vowed that next year we'd have a bigger pond, a real pond. I was hooked, and I wanted more.

On the day we brought them inside, I could only find five of our fish. "Looks like we lost one," I told the girls as I continued to dredge through the pond muck looking for Number Six, one of the two plain orange ones. He was nowhere to be found.

"Maybe a cat got him," Zora said.

The girl had my drama genes. "Could be. Could be. . . ."

The next spring, after a winter of neglect in which the "pond" was rarely topped off with water, we made a discovery. Number Six reappeared, all alone. He had made it through the sometimes-below-zero winter all alone.

The day we discovered him, Zora said, "We should name him Lucky!"

I had made good on my vow to have a proper pond, three feet deep and five feet across. I introduced the goldfish to their new, spacious digs and saw that, volume-wise, six fish didn't make a big enough splash. At the same time, a friend had been regaling us with tales of her designer carp: bubble-eye, lionhead, and shubunkin goldfish. I felt the need to go pedigreed. This time the girls and I went to the store and spent nearly four dollars apiece on five fish: one orange bubble-eye with ballooning air sacs below its eyes (a fish the girls thought very cute and I thought supremely creepy); two chubby black Japanese fantails — perfect studies of ungainly elegance; and two white, orange, and black calico shubunkins.

Two days later I discovered a black fantail and a shubunkin belly-up, gone to Davy Jones's locker. I fished them out, put them in a baggie, and the next day, feeling slightly annoyed and vaguely guilty, returned them to the store. I had in hand our guarantee and a sample of the pond water, as is required for a refund. The guilt was unfounded; the water pH tested perfect. Nevertheless, the deaths of the designer fish continued. I began to be reluctant to visit our little pond of horrors, but I wanted to be the one to find the bodies. Another shubunkin, then Bubbles the bubble-eyed, then, finally, the second black fantail, named, of course, Blacky. Rather than making multiple trips to the store, I put each tiny corpse in a baggie, then in the freezer — my makeshift fish morgue. At the end of the guarantee period, I returned them to the store, suspended in frozen Ziplock death. It was gruesome; I didn't let the children see.

The pH again tested fine, and our money was refunded. Bewildered and sad, I wondered aloud what was going on.

"We've had a *lot* of returns," said the pet shop guy. "I think with this heat, it's just too darn hard on the fish, too stressful."

My friend offered some of her baby shubunkins (hers had successfully spawned in her pond, producing a dozen *extra* fish), but I decided I wouldn't risk it. More fish souls on my conscience was something I didn't need.

"I think we should stick with the feeder fish," I told the girls.

Then, of course, the next year we bought the two koi.

As the pond filled, I reflected on the loss. Though I was sickened by the events, I still felt the good outweighed the bad. I looked at the fifteen survivors and saw Number Six. He turned out to be a she. She'd grown huge, and we renamed her Big Mama. I was sure it was she who had laid the eggs that hatched earlier that month. The babies were swimming around now, sleek and small and black. I wondered if they'd turn orange when they got bigger.

All the feeder fish made it through the winter, including one Zora had named Tangerine, an orange one, of course, with a beautiful, long white tail. The only one I had chosen had also survived. "Marilyn" (for Marilyn Manson) was decidedly gothic-looking, with black lips and markings near his head. He had grown so much, and his looks had changed so dramatically that I had to rename him. The once-black "lips" had become a pencil-thin moustache, and the head markings looked exactly like sideburns. Little Richard was *adorable*.

* * *

Before I knew it, it was summertime again. The koi had been dead for a full year, and the girls and I were in the pet store, getting Alice a new tag. Lily dragged me back to the feeder fish tank. "Look," she said, "there's a black one with orange lips."

I crouched down and admired the fish.

"My goodness," said the girl with the net. "I've never seen one with those markings." She called her co-worker over.

Zora spotted one with speckles, reminiscent of the shubunkins. Quite exotic for a feeder fish.

"Can we?" they pleaded.

We walked out with two more goldfish.

While I'd lightened up on the "we're saving their lives" routine, I liked to imagine that at least we were giving them a stay of execution. Maybe just a summer, but, hopefully, much more. A time to swim and be free, to frolic in warm sparkling days and moonlit nights, to navigate around real water lilies, and to enjoy the glimmer and company of other fish.

I hoped these new additions would have at least one more summer before heading off to that big goldfish pond in the sky. Or, maybe this time, we'd all be lucky.

# Love & Roses

"You've got to be kidding," I said to Andy as I cleared the breakfast dishes. "You can't work again this weekend."

"I have to. I have to finish this job."

"But you worked last Saturday, and the Saturday before. I can't remember the last time you spent a whole weekend at home! Come on. Don't leave me with the kids again."

Andy poured another cup of coffee. "Do you think I like working all the time? I'd rather be home with you."

It didn't feel that way. Hurt bloomed in me, and it came out in anger. "Maybe you shouldn't work for yourself. I know plenty of people who don't, and they have weekends off, vacations, even, if you can imagine that."

"I'll never work for someone else again. I like working for myself."

"And I'm left with the kids, constantly." I glared at him. "I feel like a single mom."

"Maybe you should get an outside job."

"Yeah, and you could hire a bookkeeper, and we could put the girls in daycare — and you could do half the work around here, too, cook the meals, take care of the yard, the pets, the bills. Sounds pretty sweet to me."

The situation deteriorated. We verbally smacked each other around on the issues of parenting, money-spending habits, neglected chores. My mind was a red fog of betrayal. All I could think was: *He's abandoning me again. A beautiful Saturday in May, and I'm going to be alone again with the kids.*

The fight ended with a hissed, "I hate you!" from me as I stormed out the back door and slammed it.

*It's good the girls are still asleep,* I thought, *or they would have witnessed another fine display of parental maturity.* My face flushed in shame. Contrary to my hateful words, I didn't hate Andy, and I knew he wasn't trying to hurt me. We were just stressed-out parents with a lot of responsibilities, trying to keep a roof over our heads and fighting to swim upstream in the river of life, without giving in to the more-than-occasional emotions of suffocation and isolation.

* * *

As I walked out into the garden, I didn't notice the dewy, crisp Colorado air. What I noticed was that there were a million chores outside, too. My irritation surged again, but the changed atmosphere slowly enveloped me, and, like a balm, soothed me.

I looked around and decided to work on the rustic arch I was building, a project that came about after Andy took down four small too-close-to-the-house weed trees. While I wasn't happy to see the trees go, I knew just what to do with them, how they'd fit into the scheme of our cottage garden. The day before I had dug the post holes, two feet deep in clay soil, and set the branchless trunks as posts. Today I'd work on connecting it all with the branches I'd removed.

After almost an hour of sawing, nailing, and wiring, enjoying the exertion and creation, my tension and hurts had mostly, but not totally, melted. I stepped back and admired my incomplete handiwork. How I loved rustic garden structures. The imperfection, the asymmetry, and the roughness all appealed to me because those qualities mirrored my own untamed gardening style. The arch also worked well with our DIY budget and, I think, with the style of our bungalow. I was surprised that my first arch was sturdy and pleasant to the eye. I'd never been mechanically inclined, but I had done it! I felt happier now, partially cleansed of bad feelings. I decided to go in, maybe even try to make amends. I'd finish the arch later, after I'd had time to reflect on its developing form.

As I gathered up the tools, I noticed the tall rose canes covering the side of Andy's workshop, our old one-car garage. Eyeing the brambles, I thought, with no small shame, how the dead wood outnumbered the living. Three years of intense drought and neglect had taken its toll. The shrubs, a hardy antique variety planted decades earlier by another owner, nearly screamed, "Over here! Help us!" I had a handsaw and pruners in hand, but I was gloveless and sleeveless. I looked at the house and pushed away the thought of going inside. I wasn't ready. Not yet.

Cautiously, I began with some dead canes, the ones I could safely saw without actually entering the briars. It went well. *This isn't difficult; you just have to pay close attention — I probably don't even need gloves.* The thorned old wood began to pile up in a heap. I took a deep breath and smiled. I moved in closer.

I soon earned a couple of scratches but was engaged in my work and reluctant to stop; after a few more, I began to wonder if I had a not-so-latent masochistic aspect to my personality. The scratches on my arm stung slightly, softly singing in agreement. ("You're a little weird . . . oh, yes, you are.") My mind wandered to those souls who actually enjoyed pain. I imagined the Marquis de Sade would relish the thought of gloveless rose pruning; he'd dispense with *all* the clothing. *But I'm not the Marquis. I'm just impulsive. Besides, I'm making such progress.* The truth was I wasn't ready to face my husband. If I went inside now, to a house full of family and demands, it would be hard to return to these canes — and I was so enjoying the solitude and productivity.

I squeezed in, past a gentle honeysuckle who would do me no harm. Deep in the thicket, I found myself wedged between the garage and the roses, with only a couple of feet in which to maneuver. It was darker there, like a medieval forest. The morning, still young, felt cool in the shadows, and the air fresh. Canes were beginning to leaf out, and the birds sang. It was lovely, and I began to forget about the scratches. I discovered the dead wood was especially hard and thick, and the thorns menacing. After another 10 minutes of exertion and yet another bloody scratch, I began to imagine that the thorns were consciously vicious. They resembled sharp, curved talons. Dragon's claws.

That image, wed with the romantic dappled light, conjured a fairy tale. I thought about the briars that held Sleeping Beauty's kingdom captive for one hundred years. They too were treacherous, all enclosing. I started at a sharp pain and drew back — my index finger was impaled with a large thorn. Could this be Nature's retribution for the lover's quarrel? Wincing, I pulled the thorn out, and the garnet blood made a jewel drop on my skin. I stuck the injured finger into my mouth and immediately thought of Aurora, Sleeping Beauty. Surely this is how she must have felt when pricked by the spinning wheel, the almost-premonition of a stab, then, too late, it was done. The deep sleep began. Only after a century, and numerous bloody, failed attempts by velvet-cloaked suitors, was the true prince able to enter and awaken her. The protective brambles parted only for him; he was blessed.

Moving thoughtfully now, wielding my slender saw like a sword, I focused on consideration and good thoughts for the roses — those exquisite sentinels. That is how the prince of kisses would think, I was sure of it. I did not get any more scratches.

In a short time, the canes would be covered with soft pinkish-cream buds, the baby blooms cradled and partially hidden by endearing dark green sepals. Those symbols of youth (gather ye rosebuds) would grow, swell, and open into almost luminescent-white blossoms with a spicy, lemony scent. Full blown, hardy, irresistible roses, so much like blossoming young women. Soon they'd be wide awake and ready for pollination. I thought of how, in years with rain, the canes had exploded with blooms. I had laughed out loud at the sight of greedy squirrels stuffing whole roses into their mouths. Snow-white flowers, rose-red blood. As I pruned and sawed, my mind began to make more associations between love and roses. Did roses really mean love?

Well, I thought, new love was heady, and like attar of roses, bore no comparison. Like perfume, like a dream, it could engulf us, make us unaware of the outside world, to everything but itself. New love reminded me of a selfish, pampered, hot-house tea rose, a Miss America bouquet, stripped of its thorns, nestled in tissue paper, put in a box, and wrapped with a big bow. I remembered how my husband and I once bloomed as hot and perfect as those tea roses. In our springtime, those years together before becoming parents, we had few cares and fewer thoughts of the future. We were content to revel in one another. But early love was fleeting, too precious for the rigors of time, too fragile in the face of hardship to last. Sometimes with boxed bouquets, the blossoms died before they even opened.

I recalled my horrible words earlier that morning. The thorns. The opposite of those velvety, color-soaked petals strewn on beds of love. The wounds they left were the result of the slashings of reality, the smothering trials of everyday life. I'd seen love as destroyer in my own family and in the relationships of friends. Thorns of Delusion. Delusions of who we were, who our lovers were. I had seen the thorns that destroyed a hundred years' of Aurora's suitors destroy others; I had felt them myself. A few times they had come close to destroying my own love.

"You've made quite a pile there."

Frowning at the difficulties of love, I hadn't noticed Andy had walked up and was watching me. I peered through the greenery, smiling awkwardly at the handsome king, and wiped the sweat from my brow. "Yeah, I kind of went crazy. I'm pretty scratched up, but I'm just about finished. It looks a lot better, don't you think?"

"It looks great. I'll help you get those canes in the trash."

"Really?" I wiggled out. "Thanks."

We'd apologized the way we usually did, without words. As he walked away, hauling a bundle of dead canes, I contemplated the roses I'd pruned. The hardy antique roses, with ancient, wild parentage, were built to last, so unlike the pampered hybrid teas. In fact, there were antique roses in Europe, still living, that bloomed during the time of the Brothers Grimm, and in France, Josephine's rose garden still survived. While there were never guarantees, I felt that through the stings and scrapes of life, the love I shared with this man had proved to be a variety that would insist on living and blooming, through drought and hardship, year after year, rooted deeply, tenaciously, into the soil.

# Garden Goddess for Hire

## July 3

The first three hours were business as usual; I focused on: weeding, watering, clipping, and tying rose canes to arbors, all the while enjoying the sunshine and the occasional mountain breeze.

Then boredom set in. Because I'd been reading bushels of storybooks about talking animals to Zora and Lily, it seemed natural to amuse myself by inventing tales about plants and other animated citizens of the garden.

As I crouched in the grass and dug out weeds, I imagined the Kentucky Bluegrass family were the well-fed and manicured lords and ladies of the manor. And it had made them quite uppity.

"Oh, look, it's *Mr. Dandelion*," whispered Lady Grass to her friends as she eyed the stranger standing across the ballroom. "How did *he* get in?" The ladies secretly thought Mr. Dandelion dandy, a good-natured hunk with a gorgeous yellow mane. But he was not of "their kind," so they'd never say this aloud.

Lords Blade and Spike were standing nearby. Blade smirked. "Oh, look Spike, it's *Dandelion*. You know how the Dandelions are — give them any room at all and they'll simply take over."

"Yes, and they're so garish!" said Spike. "You know, I heard the Vincas are in the process of moving. They are quality, but still, it'll be nice to have the neighborhood to ourselves again."

The ladies overheard the lords' conversation. They smiled and nodded.

I dug out Mr. Dandelion with my apple green Martha Stewart trowel. He took it like a weed. Didn't say a thing.

"Sorry," I said, before I tossed him next to the vincas I'd removed from the lawn and potted.

In the hole created by Dandelion's departure, I spied two worms. Even they were insufferable snobs.

"You're a *Broadmoor* worm, son, act like it!" said Big Daddy Squiggles.

Sonny Boy Worm stretched tall, trying to make it appear that he had a spine.

Everyone knew their place here in the Broadmoor, our city's most moneyed and most pampered burg. The Broadmoor, home of the five-star, world famous hotel of the same name, had been Colorado Springs' mecca of East Coast gentility since shortly after the town was founded in the once-wild 1870s West. It was nestled next to Cheyenne Mountain, and the hotel had a new fence around it, to keep out the riff-raff. That would include me. I'm no one special. Just the hired help. A gardener.

I soon grew bored with the play, yet I was still mostly content, deep in a blissful sun/weeding trance.

The spell vanished as loud arguing came from the mansion.

A male voice declared, "I only said I found her *moderately* attractive."

The female's reply was garbled.

Who were they talking about? I guessed someone like a secretary, and I was uncomfortable to hear a domestic row. Then I imagined that perhaps the argument was about *me*. After all, there I crouched, easily visible not ten feet away from their huge Palladian-style windows, trimmed down and toned considerably from weeks of physical labor, brown as a berry, healthy, flushed with sweat and sunshine, feeling creative and a little sexy. Perhaps, I mused, my cleavage was visible as I tended the grass. Maybe the Mr. had a wondering eye, and the Mrs. was quite fed up with it.

My mind drifted again, and I recalled where I had gotten the idea that I might be the subject of the couple's fight. Recently I had seen the film *Gods and Monsters*. In it, the director of *Frankenstein* fame lusted after Clay, "the yard man," played by Brendan Fraser. The old tomcat watched Clay from *his* window, greedily and secretly lapping him up, like so much yard man cream. Soon Clay was invited in for a glass of iced tea, then lunch, then he received an offer for a modeling job; posing nearly nude for a painting.

My lingering bit of zen faded. I began to feel as trapped as the yard man did in Queen Leer's studio, but in another way. I missed the girls, who were at home with Andy. I was tired of working in the heat every day, waiting for my skin to shrivel up like a dried peach. My own garden was seriously neglected, and an idea I had for a YA novel begged to get out on paper. I was sick of working in spoiled people's gardens, amusing myself by having the plants perform, making up sexy gardener scenarios. I was bored out of my mind. I had been almost since I started this work.

\* \* \*

I'd been playing professional gardener for nearly three months. Becky, who had been left short-handed that April, had asked me to come work for her part time, only fifteen to twenty hours a week. I'd jumped at the chance. Getting out of the house, having a break from domesticity, was a plus, as was having a "real" (read "paying") job. I welcomed the opportunity for camaraderie, outdoor work, and extra cash with which to indulge my own garden. Now I was having second thoughts.

But I should tell the story from the beginning. . . .

### April 18th

Becky picked me up on the first day in her small truck, the back of it covered with ecology-minded bumper stickers and hippie words of wisdom, including: "Who Owns You?" "Subvert the Dominant Paradigm," "Dare to Legalize Drugs," and "Trees are the Answer." Becky, who I had met in Master Gardener classes, was 10 years older than I, in her forties, and I had become one of her greatest admirers. I saw her as an individual in a city where marching to the tune of your own drummer was frowned upon, a city run by special interests, which included fundamentalist Christians, the military, and developers, to name three.

Becky spent much of her free time on environmental awareness — promoting permaculture, helping to save wild spaces.

She was also involved in non-environmental causes, such as helping the poor. After I joined the Manitou Springs Garden Club, I learned that, like me, Becky was a writer. We had become good friends.

Becky also fit into the category of "Early Hippie," and she looked the part, with nearly waist-length, beginning-to-grey hair braided in a ponytail and covered with a floppy straw hat. Today she wore a tie-dye tank top, Teva sandals, and dangling jewelry of silver and wood.

On our first day working together, we headed to the nursery to pick up some feather meal, a deer repellent. Becky bantered with the help at the counter as I took it all in, happy to be part of a new adventure.

As we pulled out of the driveway, she spied the seashell-shaped top of a birdbath, lying near a fence. It was chipped on one side. "Oh, look at that!"

"Garden art," I said.

"I'm going to go ask them about it."

I waited in the truck. The birdbath was a throwaway, and she claimed it. Back in the cab, Becky smiled and said, "Bitchin'."

Becky rescued more than birdbath tops; as a foster mom for plants, her home garden was filled with orphans that came from trash bins and compost piles.

At the first client's home, I met Becky's new business partner, a 22-year-old. Becky had filled me in about Tamara on the way over — she was a former high school valedictorian, taking some time off from college. She'd just bought her own home, a small ranch-style house. Becky discovered her last year, working for eight dollars an hour for another gardener. When that gardener moved out of state, Becky snagged Tamara. "I could not believe how much she knew," Becky told me earlier in the truck. "She's a genius."

I felt more than a tinge of envy when I heard about all of the young gardener's accomplishments. I asked Becky if Tamara had completed Master Gardener certification and learned that she hadn't been accepted to the program, yet. *Well, at least I have that on her*, I thought.

Tamara had met us in the driveway when we arrived. With her short blond hair pulled into a ponytail, she looked younger than I had imagined. She wore a big smile and no makeup. The first thing Becky did was comment on Tamara's pretty feet. I looked down, and yes, they were pretty in her sandals, and with painted toenails, too. I couldn't help but think how my own feet, that I'd always liked just fine, and even thought were cute, would not win any beauty contests. They were sturdy and thick in the ankles, like the Tahitian girls in Gaugin's paintings. Today they were clad in my usual gardening footwear, Converse.

"Man, the *nepeta*'s seeded everywhere," Tamara said as she looked around the yard. "Also the asters. We'll need to work on that today. There's also tons of ash tree seedlings."

"Ah, the asters." Becky winked at me. "I call 'em pain-in-the-asters."

I found that while Tamara delighted in letting plant-Latin roll effortlessly off her tongue, she also spoke Slanglish; she said "bitchin'" a lot, like Becky, but her favorite expression was "killer," as in "those were some killer *pachysandra*."

The two of them were obviously tight. They both wore those Teva sandals and carried matching Hori-Hori knives (which Tamara said she ordered through *Horticulture* magazine) in their matching ladies' size leather tool belts. I couldn't help but be a little envious of their relationship.

The client's home was palatial, with huge, water-sucking lawns of green, lush Kentucky bluegrass, which I found deplorable in our time of drought. Flowers and shrubs bordered the lawn on all sides, and a tree-filled wild area stretched out at the back of the property. Becky said she'd found bear poop out there before, and, last spring, a swarm of bees clinging to a tree branch. She also said it was a good place to squat and pee if you have an emergency.

I pondered that for a millisecond and thought, *I don't think so.* While I wasn't fearful of wildlife, I didn't want to be spied pissing in someone's backyard.

We spent four hours weeding.

The end of the morning found us on top of a stuccoed cement wall, pulling up ash tree seedlings.

"Damn, this bra is killing me," Becky said, tugging at the bottom of it. "Women shouldn't be trussed up like turkeys."

When I got home I felt good, but tired. Spending most of the day in the fresh air had been wonderful.

## April 20

On my third day out, I worked for another gardener. Kate was Becky's friend, a brilliant garden designer. She asked Becky if she could spare someone, and Becky asked if I was interested. I knew Kate and I liked her a lot; I said sure.

We labored hard at a beautiful Victorian hotel, beginning with planting five-gallon shrubs all morning long.

The second task was climbing to the top of a 16' ladder, with 30-pound, 5-gallon buckets of soil. We dumped the soil at the top of the wall the ladder leaned on, to enrich the new planting area. Heights-neurotic that I am, the prospect of doing this terrified me; luckily one of the younger workers, a British girl, didn't mind standing on the ladder while we brought the buckets to her. By the time we left, the fair-haired Brit had a nasty sunburn.

At the end of the day, Kate told me that she'd pay me the same 15 dollars per hour that Becky paid me, but only for today. She said she'd love for me to work for her again, but in the future she could only offer 12 dollars an hour. She confided that the other women working for her, including one who was over 40 and had to drive 60 miles round trip each day, received only 10 dollars an hour for this back-breaking/no benefits/no healthcare work.

With no hard feelings, I realized that, to Kate, I wasn't doing anything the untrained couldn't do. The saddest part was 12 dollars an hour wasn't a bad wage for this work, in this city, but it was a survival-only wage. As a subcontractor, I had to go where the money was, and it wouldn't be worth it to work for Kate again.

## April 22

I worked with the whole crew: Becky, Tamara, and two younger women who also worked part time, usually on the days I was off. We crawled over a high, rounded garden bed near a driveway and filled in the few bare spots with new perennials. I'd only been a professional gardener for a couple of weeks, so I was still self-conscious. I regularly asked Becky how she did things.

The plants we put in were bigger than usual, quart size. We moved the thick mulch and dug the holes. There was always a significant mound of soil next to the newly planted addition, in a little pile beside the mulch.

"What should I do with all the extra soil?" I asked. I realized it was a stupid question, but couldn't help myself, everything was so meticulously groomed.

Becky laughed out loud. "I'm going to give you a Native American name, 'Extra Soil.' Just smooth it around."

Later she told me how happy she was that I was working for her. She complimented everyone on a daily basis and referred to us all as gardening goddesses. It was the first time I'd experienced this behavior in a "boss" (a word that Becky hated), and it felt good.

## April 24

Becky didn't usually pick me up until 9:00 A.M., at the earliest, and we didn't usually get to the first garden until after 9:30. I hated getting to the job so late. It felt like I wasn't getting enough done at home in the morning, and then, by the time I got home in the afternoon, I was worn out. I'd prefer to go out early in the morning when it was cooler, but Becky said the clients didn't like us to arrive until after 9:00. *La dee da*, I thought, *who cares about the gardeners working in the heat?*

Becky and I dug a new bed together at a home I hadn't worked at before, a house they called the "Pink House" because the owner had a preference for pink flowers.

I asked Becky about rabbit hutches. Andy was building one for Zora and Lily's new rabbit, Oscar, and I wondered about size. Becky had been keeping rabbits for years. She rhapsodized about bunny manure; it was the best, she said. Low in nitrogen, it could be put right on the garden soil and wouldn't burn plants.

"He should make it big," she said about the hutch, as she popped a dandelion out of the ground.

"It is." I ripped out a bindweed vine.

"*Real* big." She grinned. "A big ass hutch."

I laughed and echoed her, "Yeah, a big ass hutch." We snickered together under our straw hats, *Heh hehheh*, the female Beavis and Butt-head of the horticultural world.

I bought one of the leather tool belts, trying to fit in with Becky and Tamara, I suspect, but I didn't like it. Every time I crouched down, a tool poked or jutted out at me. And, as a person who won't leave home without at least some makeup on, it felt too butch. I went back to carrying my tools in a bucket and leaving them scattered like rose petals around the job site.

## May 10

I edged a huge flower bed, going along with a shovel, slicing out pieces of sod that had crept in too close, shaking out the grass from the soil, making a pile of *Pennisetum* for the compost pile. The owner disliked black plastic lawn edging so it all had to be done manually. Becky reminded me to switch legs periodically and told me how she blew out one of her knees with the shovel work.

I enjoyed the gardening, but I could honestly say I wasn't too impressed with the neighborhood. While I admired much of the architecture and all of the beauty, everything seemed too big, much too big, for so few people. As a child, I had experienced poverty between the ages of seven and ten. For a few years after my mom and dad divorced, my 23-year-old mom, my three younger siblings, and I survived on welfare. We drank reconstituted powdered milk and ate "gov't" cheese and canned shredded chicken, foods that I would never be able to eat again as they made me think of those days. Once, through a charity, we received Christmas presents that included a used stuffed animal, a donkey. The donkey was adorable, but I remember being repulsed. It smelled like someone else's house. Spending a winter using an outhouse and bathing in a metal tub next to a fireplace is something that only sounds romantic. And I've never, ever forgotten what poverty felt like.

### May 12

I planted annuals (salvia, petunias, lobelia, and dusty miller) in a built-in planter at the top of a ten-foot-tall brick wall. The planter could only be reached by ladder. My fear of heights kicked in again, and I was a little shaky, but I went about my business. A few minutes after I started planting, I saw a bee fly into a small hole in a brick below me. She left, then returned, and I moved down to get a closer look. The bee carried a perfectly round piece of leaf. I kept tabs on her as she came out again and flew away.

By the time she returned I was very close, my face about a foot away from the hole. I wasn't worried about being stung, as I knew she was working and not concerned at all with me. As she positioned herself for a landing, I got a micro-view. She held the leaf with her thin, long-for-a-bee, legs. The leaf was partially rolled up, so it'd fit in the hole. I watched her as she hovered for a few more moments, wings beating rapidly. She was about the same size as a honeybee, stout and hairy, with a metallic blue cast. She completely ignored me, so intent she was on her work. It was like a TV nature show, a micro-view of one infinitesimal part of nature, but a million times better. It was the coolest thing I had ever witnessed in a garden.

Becky told me later I'd seen a leafcutter bee. They cut precise circles and ovals to line the bottom and sides of their long, tunnel-like nests. They create small cells, lay one egg per cell, provision each with a mixture of nectar and pollen, and cap the cell with another circle of green.

"When you see rose leaves with these perfect holes in them, it's the leafcutter," Becky said. "They cause some damage, but not enough to get worked up about. What's really cool about it all, is that the first egg they lay, the oldest one in the far back of the tunnel, is the last to hatch and come out."

I admired the leafcutter for her industriousness. Later, I looked her up on the internet and discovered the *Megachile* species are important native pollinators in the western United States. They are not aggressive, they have a mild sting (milder than honeybees and wasps), and they are only a threat when handled. Our Colorado entomological expert, Whitney Cranshaw, wrote: "Leafcutter bees are solitary bees, meaning that they don't produce colonies . . . Instead, individual female leafcutter bees do all the work of rearing."

## May 13

Today we worked worked on the east side of town, in an upper-middle-class neighborhood for a gynecologist. Becky referred to the doctor by her first name, Annie. Near the house, Annie's back garden held a patio and a small lawn, the running ground for two amiable terriers. It also had a koi pond that was covered with netting to protect the prize fish from the occasional blue heron. Above that was a huge rock garden, built into the surrounding hill, and made of terraced stone walls. Topping that was an upper garden of boulders and flowers, which was backed by a parched meadow. Becky said the meadow was a perfect habitat for rattlesnakes.

The temperature was in the upper 80s, warm for that time of year, so we'd been drinking a lot of water. I was thankful Annie had welcomed us to use her bathroom facilities. It meant we didn't have to drive to the nearest 7-Eleven (like we had to do when we worked in the Broadmoor).

I called this the Hades garden. On top of the rock wall, it was especially hot and dry, and our weeding work, started at opposite ends of the garden, had over the course of two hours brought us together. We squatted at the top of the property, among the

84

delphinium, yucca, lupine, and soon-to-be scorching boulders. I was the first to finish, and when I stood up my head swam.

"Whoa," I said, "I just got a head rush."

Becky and Tamara found this amusing.

"She just got a twirly," said Tamara.

"Congratulations," said Becky. "Having a twirly is one of the milestones in becoming a gardener."

After some shrub pruning, we gathered our tools to leave. Becky pointed out a red-tailed hawk that soared above us in the cloudless sky, and I wondered if it had also been a threat to the koi.

### May 15

One of a hired gardener's perks is keeping whatever they weed out. I always deferred to Becky and Tamara, but I'd still scored some *coreopsis*, pain-in-the-aster, *Knautia macedonica* (red pincushion flower; Becky calls them "naughty-uh" because of their fecundity), hollyhocks, and even a tiny tree — an *Arborvitae* Becky potted up personally and presented to me.

Becky nurtured the orphans in her own garden and gave them to garden club members and to the church where we held our monthly garden club meetings. Most of the time, though, she relocated them to another of her clients' gardens as freebies. I was astonished at her non-capitalistic attitude and didn't think I'd be so generous.

### May 18

Today we met the garden club members at a nursery/ greenhouse. Becky was multi-tasking, picking out annuals for both our club's plant sale and for her clients. I felt thrilled to indulge in my all-time favorite gardening task, shopping. I bought several flats at wholesale prices, an orgy of annuals.

Becky and Tamara chose a truckload for their clients. Tamara raved over some parti-colored petunias, hot pink and white, white and dark purple. I thought the stripes made the flowers look circus-like and kind of garish but kept my opinion to myself.

Later in the day, one of Becky's favorite clients, a super nice, sixtyish woman who lived in a Spanish Colonial-style townhouse near the Garden of the Gods, went ga-ga over the petunias Tamara picked out. And I admit it, I was envious. Again.

### May 19

We spent a good part of the day at herbalist/author Tammi Hartung's nursery in Cañon City. I found myself in plant-lust mode again, thrilled to buy herbs and perennials at one dollar each for a two-and-a-half-inch pot. A big thrill was seeing *seven* different types of basil — Thai, Siam queen, African blue, globe, purple leafed, lemon, Genovese; five types of scented geraniums; and oh, so much more!

Becky wore short shorts and a tank top, her hair up in a ponytail. She said she was trying to even out her "gardener's tan," which is similar to the farmer's version. Becky's legs were gorgeous, and her impressively-sized breasts, I'd guessed "DD," were, like mine, slightly more on the side of Venus of Willendorf than Venus de Milo. She wasn't wearing a bra that day because she wasn't seeing any clients. When away from work, Becky didn't give a damn if she drew attention; she was freedom incarnate. I admired her uninhibited, I-know-I'm-beautiful attitude, one that I could only achieve when under the influence of a significant amount of alcohol. On more than one occasion, I'd heard her refer to herself as a "primitive," and once she told me she would love to live an aboriginal life.

That evening she called to get my hours (special note: she also paid on time). We bitched about the sprawl in Colorado Springs, and she made a comment about the developers who run our city government, "That's their job. Sucking up beautiful places and spitting out shit."

### May 20

In the afternoon we went to a new location, a huge home in a gated community. We were met by Becky's whole crew, plus two more, an older man and woman Becky hired specifically for the occasion. Our job would be planting a truckload of gallon-sized stop-sign red geraniums.

We toured the conifer garden, which was expansive and sculptural with only a few flowers. Becky called the owner by her first name, Madeline. Madeline was whip-thin, and her pretty, somewhat waxy features remind me of a well-preserved orchid, a prom-queen from ages past. Becky said she was sure Madeline had had plastic surgery. She told me that Madeline was not a gardener, but a *designer*, which meant she did all the shopping and directing of where-to-put-what. She'd given Becky some of her expensive cast-offs, purchases she'd decided she "didn't quite like" once they were in her garden.

This was the first garden I'd visited that bespoke major design savvy. Madeline's garden was Asian-influence-done-right. Every tree, shrub, and flower was carefully placed, meticulously groomed and pampered. It was the antithesis of how Becky and I rolled; we tended toward the "wild and wooly" as Becky called it. I preferred to think of it as gardening with Nature and letting Nature keep the upper hand.

It wasn't long after we began planting the geraniums that I noticed Madeline and Becky holding an animated conversation.

Madeline went inside, and Becky walked over to us. She held a big plastic jar of Osmocote, the time-release fertilizer that comes in tiny beige balls, and some measuring spoons. "Have you guys been putting Osmocote in the planting holes?" she asked.

Cindy and I shook our heads. "I didn't know we were supposed to," I said.

"Well, that's what Madeline wants. We're going to have to take them all out and put a rounded teaspoonful in each hole."

I looked at the dozens of planted geraniums. "Geez," I said, "what is she, the Osmocote heiress?"

Becky said, "No," then named a popular household appliance. "She's *that* heiress."

## May 22

We went to Mike's. Mike was a she, the 60-something widow of a military officer. She was kind of brusque, but I liked her. I was in love with her garden. It was on a hillside, had incredible diversity, and was xeric. I saw a lot of plants that I hadn't seen in other gardens and coveted the bronze Buddha nestled among poppies. I learned Mike's middle-aged son lived with her, as did two small, barking terriers. Becky left Cindy and me there to weed for three hours.

My friend Susan called that evening and asked if I'd like to do a gardening job for a friend of hers, an elderly lady who lived downtown. The woman had a Spanish Colonial-style house with a built-in planter running the entire length of her property that needed to be filled with annuals. Susan usually did the job, but she was too busy. Did I want the work?

Indeed, I did. I had my very first contract job!

## May 23

We spent the morning spreading mulch. I got to the job at 9:30 and waited 20 minutes for Becky and the crew. I was irritated, thinking about how I could have been at home, working in my own garden instead of sitting there not getting paid and knowing I would be working well into the 90-degree afternoon.

When Cindy pulled up, the owner of the home came out and greeted us.

A rake-thin, middle-aged man, he led us up the long driveway to the house. On the way, among the border of shrubs and trees, I spied a foot-tall sapling. It was a Siberian elm, the most notorious weed tree in these parts. Reflexively, I reached down and pulled it out.

The owner stopped and turned to face me. Scowling, he demanded, "Why did you do that?"

"It was a weed tree."

The next words were spoken coldly and very slowly, as if he were instructing a child: "I would appreciate it if you didn't remove anything without my *permission*."

I seethed in silence, thinking, *Here I am, a master gardener with a bachelor's degree, getting chewed out for plucking a damn weed.*

The job didn't get any better. The truck of mulch arrived — as did Becky, Tamara, and a woman I'd never met — just as it started getting nice and toasty. The wheelbarrow assembly line began. We took turns standing on the truckload of mulch to pitchfork the barrows full and then pushed the barrows up the long, steep driveway, around to the back of the house and through the trees, to dump and spread among a stand of white pines.

Back and up, back and up, over and over. It took us two hours at a fast clip, and I lost count of how many trips we made. It was fun in a way because we kind of got into this competitive thing, where we were hustling, passing each other like we were in a relay, grinning — "Hey, look at me. Top this!"

I kept asking Cindy if she was okay; her face looked so red I was worried she might pass out, but Becky said mine was the same. "Are you Irish?" she asked Cindy. Cindy didn't understand at first and thought it may have been a put-down, about liking to drink or something, but then Becky said it was a Celtic trait — to get so obviously flushed when exerted. I learned that she was of Celtic origin too.

Meanwhile, The Marquis de Sod, Supreme Protector of Weed Trees, stood in the shade, watching four attractive, dressed-for-summer women haul wheelbarrows of mulch up and down his driveway, nearly collapsing from heat exhaustion. I sensed he was enjoying himself.

## May 24

The side job for the lady downtown worked out perfectly. I spent Saturday morning buying plants and soil amendment and finished planting that afternoon. It was fun, and I made a nice profit. I felt it was so much better being the boss, no matter how perfect your boss was.

It was a new week, and we had a new client. Another garden in the Broadmoor. This home had construction going on; a new wing was being added to the thousands of square footage already in existence. We weeded and planted annuals.

As Becky and I drove homeward in her truck, we debated the differences between garden tours in her artsy-fartsy, celebrating-diversity town, Manitou Springs, where most of the gardeners were the sole garden workers and designers, and the gardens in the Broadmoor. Our garden club's tour was coming up and would feature gardens tended by the club's professional gardeners. Most of those gardens were in the Broadmoor.

"The difference," Becky said, "is that up there you get to see what shitloads of money can do for a garden."

"Hmmm," I said. "Maybe we should call it the 'Shitloads of Money Tour.'"

The day before, Becky said that if we had a serious job we'd probably get into trouble.

## May 31

The hottest May in the city's recorded history was drawing to an end, and, according to forecasts, June was also going to be a scorcher. Becky said global warming had been obvious for years to those who work out in nature. I told her that for years I had been reading editorials in our local paper that global warming was a hoax. We both shook our heads.

I got up early, while everyone else was still sleeping, to water some plants in my own garden and to let the chickens out while the morning was dewy and cool. As I walked by my handmade arbor, I saw a honeybee, damp and dew-covered, crawling out of a poppy. I'd heard that if bees were gathering nectar and pollen and it got too late to return to the hive, they'd sleep in a flower, but I'd never seen it. She'd been slumbering and was unable to fly away until she'd dried. I felt blessed to witness this.

I worked that morning alone, removing a big patch of 'King Alfred' daffodils. Becky wanted me to save the bulbs, and she gave me trash bags to put them in.

The 'King Alfreds' were deeply embedded in muck. I couldn't believe they were down so deep, over a foot, and that the ground was *so frigging wet*. Every time I put the shovel in to pry them out, there was a tremendous sucking sound and the gigantic mound resisted me. It felt like the bulbs were stuck in glue, that I was in a bog. Soon I wore platform-mud heels and was cursing under my breath. I was offended thinking of how much water the garden was using with our community deep in drought! And this garden wasn't the only one. Not by a long shot. When I saw Becky again, I told her about the experience, with the instruction, "Don't *ever* send me on a job like that again." She found it hilarious.

In the heat of the afternoon we went to the Hades garden. At one point, Becky accidentally broke off a daylily bud.

"Darn," she said, popping the bud into her mouth. "Yum."

Before we left, Becky dusted everything, not with fairy-dust, but with feather meal, a deer-repellant that Becky said was made of "chicken parts." I had never smelled anything so god-awful in my life — it was worse than shit, worse than skunk, worse than fish emulsion; it was like the ground-up, rotting entrails of the vilest sea/land/air creatures imaginable. I couldn't see how Becky bore it.

On the way home, Becky stopped at a 7-Eleven to wash up and asked me if I needed anything. When she came back to the truck, she had a paper container holding a corn dog, dripping in nacho cheese sauce product. "Sorry," she said, "but I was starving."

## June 4

Becky sent me to Mike's alone. As Mike showed me where to work, I commented on a *Salvia argentea*, a huge, hairy-leafed, silver plant now at its rosette stage. Mike said, "Oh, Monty bought that." She said it in a dismissive way that bothered me, the same tone she used when I commented on some interesting pavers that Monty bought. I thought it was cool that her son was into gardening and felt sort of sorry for him, that his mom was so prickly.

I weeded for a couple of hours in the 90-plus degree heat, then took a thirty-minute lunch break for an iced cappuccino. I walked into the coffee shop filthy, covered in dirt and sweat, but I felt good, fully endorphin-ized by the sun and work.

Mike offered me two pass-along plants to take home, some orange hawkweed I was digging out of her beds, and some other weed, a type of malva. "The only name I know it by is "devil's paintbrush," she said of the hawkweed. "I brought it from back East, where it grows wild all over the place. They say it's a terrible weed, but it's easy to pull up. I don't think it's bad at all." The plant had a low, mounded, hairy-leafed base with thin ten-inch stems that shot up and were topped by a burnt orange flower cluster. It was sculptural, interesting. Mike resembled the flower's base, short, stocky, with short hair. She was interesting, too, but, like the weed, difficult to interpret.

She came out to tell me when it was time to leave and seemed concerned when I didn't pack up right away. I finished the area I was in 10 minutes later, and didn't mark it on my card, figuring it would be a nice way to show my gratitude for the pass-alongs. It had been a lonely morning in a stranger's garden, but I was excited about the free weeds.

Zora and Lily had been out of school for almost a week, and though I longed for them, they hardly missed me at all. They were having a grand time hanging out with their Dad, and he with them. The house was about at the same stage of decay as it normally was, so I couldn't even claim things were going to hell without me. I felt like they were having a party that I wasn't invited to.

### June 8

The crew spent the morning at the name-brand heiress's home. I heard her and Becky argue twice. The first time was over some perennials Madeline bought through mail-order from an expensive East Coast nursery.

They were standing over the tiny plants that Becky and Tamara planted personally two weeks before. Madeline said, "I just don't understand why they're not doing better."

"Madeline, they're fine," said Becky. "They've only been in the ground two weeks. They have to establish their root system in the new soil before they'll start having top growth."

This did not please the heiress. "They're just so small. I'm not happy with them."

"You could have bought bigger plants locally, for less money," said Becky, and I cringed because I knew it wasn't going to go over well. It was Becky's buy-local-think-global policy; she wasn't able to resist. "And they would have been acclimated too."

Madeline tossed her well-coiffed head. "I suppose."

Later, when it was almost time to leave, Becky introduced me to Madeline as "a Master Gardener." This pleased Madeline, and she smiled graciously, as did I. I returned the Osmocote to the potting shed and ran to the back garden to look for my bypass pruners. Two minutes later I was back, and the ladies were still standing in the driveway.

"I buy them small, because when you buy a smaller plant, you're going to have a healthier plant," I heard Becky explain. I noticed the object of the conversation was a gallon-sized plant she held in one hand, a foot-tall lavender-flowered clematis that was planted earlier in the trellised area near the driveway.

"I would just like a bigger one," said Madeline.

"It won't take that long for it to grow, once it becomes established," Becky insisted. "I guarantee you it will catch up." She smiled at Madeline, and I could see she'd decided to turn on her considerable charm. "Now, what would you rather have, a healthier plant or instant gratification?"

The pause wasn't as long as a gnat's ass. "Instant gratification," Madeline said. She smiled back at Becky when she said it, then looked over at me, and, in spite of myself, I felt a naughty (and guilty) admiration for her swagger. Becky looked dejected.

In the truck, Becky told me that Madeline was having all the perennials she special-ordered from some "Fancy East Coast Flower Farm" pulled out. She was seething.

When I got home it was plain to see that Zora and Lily had a great day with their dad. It was as if I hadn't spent the previous decade of my life being their personal entertainment center and doting, loving, 24/7 mama. And I'd recently read them *all* the Harry Potter books! Andy's dinner was very good, too.

## June 10

Tamara and I got into a disagreement over a plant identification at one of her gardens. She'd been bounding around happily for the previous two hours, fine tuning while I weeded, like she was in a personal paradise she created with one hand tied behind her back. Again, I felt envy. She was younger, in charge, and didn't have children to pine for while she worked. She identified a plant as fernleaf yarrow; I said it was tansy. The plant wasn't in bloom. I remarked on the pungent foliage and smartly shared my knowledge that the word tansy came from the French word for "nose-twister." I had one in my yard.

"It's a fernleaf yarrow!" Tamara was exasperated, and I felt satisfied that I'd irritated her. This wasn't like me. I could be bitchy, but never this argumentative and resentful. What the hell was wrong with me?

I looked up the plant that evening. Tamara was right, it was fernleaf yarrow.

My feelings for Tamara were mixed. I liked her and, for no rational reason, I didn't. She seemed to have all the answers, her compass confidently pointing toward business ownership and independence at such a young age. I, on the other hand, was rapidly approaching middle age and didn't know where the hell I was headed, though I was beginning to worry I might have an entire life of scraping by and not knowing what, aside from mothering, I was supposed to be doing.

Andy had teased me numerous times about my apparent inability to settle on anything. I had investigated becoming an interior designer, tried my hand at journalism, and thought about opening a tea shop. Doctor, lawyer, Indian chief. I couldn't figure out what I was meant for. I loved writing and gardening more than anything (other than mothering), and yet so many other subjects held me in rapt fascination. Besides this, I was beginning to realize that the girls were growing older and we all needed more independence. I knew I shouldn't cling too tightly, but at the same time I knew those childhood years wouldn't last, and I didn't like being away from my girls.

To me, Tamara seemed lucky. She knew more about gardening than I did and even had the good fortune to be raised by gardeners. Not only her mom, but grandma too! I had to learn it all on my own. No one to guide me down the primrose path. I suspected Becky liked Tamara better too — how could she not? My truthful side told me I was being a jerk.

## June 13

We went to a surgeon's home, and it was one of the most beautiful gardens so far. In the backyard was a pool and bursting, blooming, lovely English cottage-style beds all around, designed and planted by the missus, a highly-educated, likeable, down-to-earth woman. She chatted with us and I learned she enjoyed shopping at Walmart and Home Depot for plants. That stopped me. All this and . . . *Walmart? Wow*, I thought. *She's the opposite of the franchise queen.* Becky and I refused to shop at Walmart, knowing that low prices for some came at a steep price for others, namely American businesses, Walmart employees, and taxpayers.

The garden would have been a glorious place to weed, indeed, except for one thing. There was dog poop everywhere, compliments of an obese golden retriever who stayed in his kennel while we were there. (His imprisonment was required because he had an excitable nature — we were told that if loose, we'd all be humped.) I felt concerned that something was definitely amiss with that dog because his urine, which was everywhere, reeked.

As I weeded, gingerly avoiding turds, longing for a tussy-mussy to hold to my nose, I wondered at the mess. I was far from fastidious, but this was beyond even my level of tolerance. *Surely if these people can afford three gardeners at 20 dollars an hour apiece,* I thought, *they can afford to hire someone to pick up the dog shit.*

At another garden, one of the tasks included braiding daffodil foliage. The flowers were wilted and gone, and the long, green leaves of the daffodils were floppy and, I supposed, unattractive. Yet the bulb needed the energy garnered from those green leaves, so the leaves couldn't be cut off. I felt absolutely ridiculous braiding daffodil foliage. For some reason it reminded me of extravagant pubic-hair grooming, like when a friend told me she had her pubic hair trimmed into a heart shape for her boyfriend in celebration of Valentine's Day. *Not* my thing.

### June 15

We were in Hades again, weeding together in a group, Becky, Tamara, and I. Like May, June was turning out to be the hottest on record, and we were getting extremely bitchy.

Becky asked me, "What's your astrological sign?"

"Capricorn."

"Oh, *Capricorn*," she said, lifting an eyebrow. "My mom's a Capricorn; I know all about *you*." Her tone was definitely on the smart-alecky side, with the tiniest hint of hostility, and I wondered what she was getting at. She'd mentioned she and her mom had been at odds many times, over religion, politics, and life in general.

"Well, what's yours?" I asked.

"Libra."

*Well, I'll be damned,* I thought. My mom was a Libra, and I could see similarities between her and Becky. My Mom and I were often at odds, too. What a coincidence. In that moment it seemed to me that Becky shared my mother's most annoying habits.

"Ha," I said, "I know all about *you*, too."

### June 17

A good day. I caught my first snakes *and* was stung by a wasp. Maybe that doesn't sound fun, but for me, Mrs. Wild at Heart, it was exciting. Both events occurred at The Rennick's, a house with another big rock wall garden, two doors down from Hades. I dubbed it Hades II. That morning, I spotted a yellow jacket and told Tamara. Becky said it was probably nesting in the wall, and the owner would spray because yellow jackets were aggressive. To confirm this, within two minutes I was stung, and endured a white-hot sensation on my wrist, but only for a few minutes. I felt rather proud of my ability to endure wasp-venom.

An hour later I noticed a snake.

Tamara was nearby so I called her attention to it.

"It's a ribbon snake," she said. "Get it."

Not thinking, I reached out and grabbed. My gloved hand came back with two snakes, one about a foot long and the other a few inches smaller, both brilliant green with yellow stripes. My heart lurched, but I didn't squeal.

Luckily, Tamara had the weed bucket ready and I dropped them in. They slithered up the bucket's sides, frantically trying to escape. Watching them, I squirmed.

"Grab some weeds," ordered Tamara. I gathered some up from the drying pile on the lawn and dropped them over the snakes. They chilled out.

"See, they just wanted some cover."

"Woo-wee!" said Becky, who'd joined us.

Tamara left to get a shirt to tie over the top of the bucket with a bungee cord.

"My God," I said. "I've never even held a snake before. It's a good thing I had gloves on, or I couldn't have done it."

Becky chuckled. "Your eyes were pretty big. Tamara will take them home and put them in her garden. It's not a good idea to have them here. Annie, next door, is terrified of them, and if her boyfriend sees them, he'll kill them. He's done it before."

"But these are ribbon snakes," I said. "They're *beneficial*."

Becky arched her eyebrows. "Tell that to someone standing on a lawn chair, screaming. Oh, by the way, sweetie, you've completed the second milestone that certifies you as a true gardener — snake rescue."

I felt a new kinship with Tamara. I would have loved to take the snakes home, but my chickens probably would have made a meal out of them.

## June 20

We'd been working in the Shitloads of Money area all morning when Tamara arrived with another gardener. Her goofy, very-pleased-with-it-all attitude was so much lighter than the usual Tamara. When I noticed that she was admiring a bush clematis a little too much, I started to suspect she'd been smoking Mother Nature.

A half-hour later I heard bells playing, "You're a Grand Old Flag."

"Where's that coming from?" I asked Becky.

"Oh, it's the carillon in the church, up on the hill. It plays each noon."

"Does it always play that song?"

Becky rolled her eyes. "Sure does."

The extra-happy gardener walked by. "Wow," Tamara said. "Isn't that something?"

"You should have heard it earlier," I said. "They played 'Dude Looks Like A Lady.'"

"Really?"

Tamara was *so stoned*. I was practically bubbly with a feeling of superiority. I would never arrive at a client's house in such a condition . . . though, wait, I remembered smoking pot with my boss once, at Tamara's age, at work. And, oh yeah, I also got pretty intoxicated with that same boss and a co-worker during a lunch celebration on my 21st birthday. *Perhaps*, I thought, *I should lose the smugness.*

### June 21

I called a city office about getting a license for my own gardening business and found my second freelance job. The woman I spoke to said, "You're a gardener? I need one." We set an appointment. As with the other job, I didn't tell Becky or Tamara. I wanted to test the waters first and I didn't want them to see me as a competitor.

### June 24

I was at Mike's again, by myself, on yet another 90-degree-plus day. I thought about naming the garden Hades III. After I did quite a bit of weeding, Mike's son dropped by and said hi. He seemed to be a nice middle-aged guy, cute but a little doughy. Mike had me cut down the poppies and told me I could save the decorative seed heads if I wanted. Then she went into the house. I was performing this task near sliding glass doors and had the distinct and creepy feeling that I was being watched.

The last thing I did was put up a trellis and try to attach the incredible mess of a honeysuckle vine that was spread out all over the ground. It was the first time I'd dealt with something like that, and I did the best I could, wrestling with the son-of-a-seed, but it ended up looking far from perfect. I worked past the allotted time, too, and again, I didn't record it; Mike was a nice lady, and I just wanted to complete the task.

Becky called me that night and said Mike didn't want me to come over anymore; she requested another gardener. She said I took too long to cut down the poppies. I was stunned. I'd never been fired from a job in my life. I didn't dawdle. I wondered what happened. Did it irritate her that I liked her son's contributions to the garden, or did she assume I had charged her for the extra time I spent there, or did I spend too much time admiring her flowers? (I didn't think so.) I did know Mike was hyper-aware of the time clock. I decided I probably just wasn't nose to the grindstone enough. Or, maybe, I didn't "know my place."

After some major smarting and feeling a bit hurt, I realized I couldn't waste time caring about this. I was still happy about Mike's gift of free plants.

The client/service thing was really getting under my skin. As a stay-at-home mom, I'd gone nearly a decade free as most can ever hope to be, and now I felt like a tiger lily stolen from the wild and crammed into a pot. I didn't like it, and I feared motherhood had ruined me for the workforce, that I'd never be any good in the rat race. Even though I knew this intolerance might signal an inevitable decline down the road, my awareness of it at the time was sweet.

### June 29

I completed my second freelance gardening job.

The client's name was Iris, which I took as a good omen, and she lived alone in a newer neighborhood in a modest-sized house. When we met, I saw that she was about 50, pretty, quite feminine; her home was tastefully furnished. I admired the rose-patterned china in her antique oak hutch. She told me she was sick of turf and wanted to start a garden but didn't know a thing about the green world. She wanted a couple of trellises with vines, a planter on her front porch filled with perennials, and a small flower bed in back. I checked out her grounds, which included a patchy weed-filled backyard and two small flower beds with feverfew seedlings and a few snapdragons. She coveted her neighbor's garden, an enclosed paradise of honeysuckle vines and roses. We visited it together.

I was unloosed to design this woman's garden. During my ecstatic shopping excursion, I bought multiples of extra-feminine flowers: pasque flower, columbine, oriental poppy, lady's mantle, 'Johnson's Blue' geranium, Siberian iris, 'Kent Beauty' oregano, pink baby's breath, 'Husker Red' penstemon, double hollyhocks, daylilies, 'Hidcote' lavender, and 'Rose Queen' salvia. To those I added several roses: a dark red and white Meidiland for her porch, a 'John Davis' climbing rose for the new bed below her deck, and a 'Fairy' polyantha for a large pot. Last, I gathered several vines: *Clematis tangutica,* Hall's honeysuckle, and a trumpet creeper, 'Madame Galen,' which would begin the softening of her fenced-in backyard. And, of course, I added bags of soil amendment.

I found a play date for the girls on Saturday so Andy could help me haul two fan trellises for the fence and two trellis panels to cover the space below her back deck. He hung them for me.

I loved this work, especially the creating part, and could see how developing my own business would be easy. The problem was, as much as I loved gardening, I loved writing, and being home, more. The seed of a green-hearted novel had been germinating in my mind these last months, and now it was demanding to be cultivated on paper. It'd been almost a month since my girls got out of school. Even part time was too much time away.

## July 3

On the day I began creating childlike scenarios of intrigue with worms, dandelions, and bluegrass (and, for the first time, admitted to myself that I was bored and lonely in this job), I took a noontime pee break at the Shitloads of Money neighborhood gas station/convenience store. I drove my seven-year-old Taurus, and as I stopped at the intersection right next to the store, an older man, about to cross the street on foot, stopped too. We looked at each other, and he waved my car on, gesturing grandly. Then, after I pulled in the parking lot he walked by and said, sarcastically, *"THANK YOU!"*

His rudeness unsettled me. Was I supposed to insist that he cross before me? *Oh no, Your Lordship, after you!* Or was he implying that I had not adequately recognized his politeness? As I dug for change in my purse for a drink, a woman pulled up at the pumps. She was young, blonde, skinny with huge boobs, in the biggest SUV money could buy this side of a Hummer. I'd come across one of the area's indigenous species, a trophy wife. She left the behemoth running while she darted into the store. It was safe in that hallowed neighborhood to leave a brand new vehicle running, door unlocked. No car thief would be so stupid or bold here, where police response was probably instantaneous. I was still angry at the jerk at the crosswalk and sorely wanted to pass it on, to yell, "*Hey, gas waster, turn off your damn engine!*"

The community toilet that we gardening ladies shared with all the gentlemen workers in the area (pool men, lawn mowing men, tree men, construction workers, etc., etc.) was half-clogged. I won't go into the disgusting details. I was afraid to flush, but near bursting, so I peed anyway, hovering. After I pulled up my pants, I pushed down the handle and moved away from the lidless toilet as fast as I could. The contents, thankfully, went down. My bile rose.

I thought, *Would it be too much for clients to offer facilities at their homes for their hired help, who are busting ass to make their lives more magically beautiful? Really, would an outhouse be too dear?* I thought about how Becky could make even an outhouse tres chic, covered with vines and roses. It would definitely be better than this communal shithole.

That afternoon at the Rennick's (a.k.a. Hades II, where I caught the snakes), I shared my idea about the outhouse. I'd temporarily gotten over my terrible mood because at this house I had some company. I wasn't all by myself, going crazy.

"Great idea," Becky said. "Only problem is, the workers would probably use it as a place to smoke pot."

I hadn't thought of that. *So, who cares?*

I bitched a little more and Becky told me that in all the years she's been a gardener, she'd never gotten so much as a card on Christmas from the Shitloads of Money crowd.

## July 8

By the second week in July, all the new installations had gone in, and the flowerpots, hanging baskets, and window boxes had been filled. The weeds were under control. Gardening had become mind-numbing maintenance. Deadheading, endless weeding. I didn't want to be a hired gardener anymore, and I was a little doubtful I would ever start my own gardening business. It was too hard physically, too hard on my ego, and I didn't like being away from my daughters, especially when they were home all day during the summer. Life — and childhood — were just too short. I told Becky I was going to leave, that I wanted to get back to writing and my family. She understood.

I was liberated!

## Postscript: February 12, the following year

I came away from my professional gardening experience with a souvenir — tennis elbow, the result of all those physically demanding tasks in the taming of the green. My right elbow ached for months afterward. I was glad it finally let up, because it was time to start looking forward to working in my own garden again.

I talked to Becky, and she said she and the heiress didn't make it through the summer. The green grind also took its toll on Tamara; she enrolled in nursing school at the end of the season. Becky said Tamara was able to make enough to live on by waitressing a few nights a week. Waitressing — even more of an expression of servitude, but one that was so much more lucrative! I felt sorry and a little guilty when I heard that things weren't nearly as rosy for Tamara as I had imagined.

Becky said she'd be looking for more crew members in a month or so. She said she thought of gardening as a profession that must also be a calling, as so many tried it and didn't stay with it. Of all the gardeners I worked with, she was the only one, to my knowledge, who had reached all the mysterious milestones of the true gardener, milestones that might forever remain unknown to me.

# Puff, the Tragic Rabbit

Puff, a.k.a. Fox Mulder, former humper-bunny extraordinaire, rested on a towel in my lap as I fed him Earth Farms Organic baby food, diluted with warm milk and spiked with crushed antibiotics. The carrot goo, administered through a syringe, dribbled out of his mouth and down his dirty-white chest. The dwarf rabbit looked rough; he'd had surgery the day before to open up a large, marble-sized abscess on his chin. We were surprised he'd made it through. I didn't see how someone so tiny and weak, little more than fur and air, could survive. I just knew his heart would give out. I'd almost planned his funeral. But here he was.

The bald, fleshy abscess now had a gaping hole in it. It was terrifically gross, but I was beginning to get used to it. I had to keep it clean by squirting it with saline solution a couple of times a day.

Even though Puff had made it through surgery, the vet hadn't been optimistic. "I wasn't able to drain it because *Lepus* have a thick, non-liquid, almost hard pus," Dr. Dormer explained, as my two daughters and I gathered around his cage. "I got out as much as I could."

Six-year-old Lily stared at the rabbit. Though she'd recently confided she thought the young doctor "cute," she wouldn't look at him now. "He's bloody," she announced, her eyes glued to Puff's blood-flecked chest. She was scandalized.

"Honey, they don't have time to bathe them after surgery," I whispered. Zora, 10, petted Puff silently.

"We'll keep him on antibiotics and see what happens," said Dr. Dormer.

As I fed Puff, I thought about the nightmare Lily shared with me that morning. She dreamed Puff had a hole in his throat and all his blood squirted out until he got as small and skinny as a deflated balloon. As he sat on my lap, sucking down baby food, wanting to live, I wanted to weep.

Maybe this was my penance for not taking good enough care of our first rabbit. Oscar was a lop-eared bunny from the feed store, the previous year's Easter present for the girls, especially Lily, who became smitten with rabbits in kindergarten. Although Oscar proved to have dangerous claws and an independent personality (in other words, not a huggable playmate), we enjoyed him as an addition to our family. Unfortunately, his stay was short. He disappeared from our fenced backyard a few months later and was never found. I'd been the one who thought it'd be okay to let him scamper free.

When spring came again, all crocuses, daffodils and marshmallow chicks, my mind returned to those happy heralds of spring, bunnies. That May, I noticed a classified ad: "Free male dwarf rabbit to a good home. Comes with a hutch and food." I called, and the owner described him: "He's Himalayan, white with dark markings."

White, I thought, *that's the rabbit color Zora likes best*. White with pink eyes, like the March Hare in *Alice in Wonderland*. Then she mentioned his name, Felix.

Felix. Our first bunny was . . . Oscar. It had to be fate.

"We want him," I said.

Less than an hour later, a winsome rabbit cuddled on my lap as Andy and I rode home in his truck. The owner said we didn't need a cage; Felix would be fine on my lap. And he was. I'd been thrilled by how damn cute he was, white with dark pearl-grey ears, muzzle and feet, and so small, only slightly bigger than a guinea pig. Only his bright pink eyes seemed strange. We were given, in addition to the bunny and hutch, a bag of rabbit pellets, mini alfalfa bales, and a salt wheel, and we were told that Felix didn't care for carrots. His owner said she'd gotten him two years ago from a sister-in-law who had, in turn, found him through an animal rescue place in Denver.

"Won't Zora be surprised?" I said, stroking the rabbit. I loved spontaneous pet buys; they weren't always the wisest, but they were, as the girls would say, the "funnest."

The girls squealed when they saw him. Zora said, "This is *exactly* the bunny I wanted!" She had a hard time choosing a new name. It was between Puff and Fox Mulder (of *The X-Files*, her favorite TV program). Lily wanted to name him Poof. I steered her away from Poof. In the weeks to follow we became so charmed with gregarious Puff, and so pleased with the Netherlands Dwarf breed, we decided to get a second rabbit for Lily. Unlike the large, lop-eared variety, Puff was manageable; his scratches didn't leave bloody gouges, and he seemed to genuinely like us. He was not, as far as I could tell, plotting a disappearance. To our surprise, when Zora offered him carrots, he loved them.

To find another bunny, I first checked with local rescue groups and the Humane Society. When those bunny trails led nowhere, I found a breeder.

The next Saturday morning, the girls and I drove to a neighborhood a few miles away and stopped at a blue house. Sadie, in her late twenties, met us at the door, all smiles. Her husband waved from the living room sofa.

From a wicker carrier by the door, Sadie brought out the bunnies, one buck and three does, so minuscule you could cradle one in the palm of your hand. Soon they bounded around the carpet. The girls and I had delighted in baby animals before — chicks, ducklings, puppies and kitties, even lambs and goats — but the five-and-a-half week old rabbits, so perfectly tiny, with cunning satin ears, velvet coats, and spun-sugar whiskers, were paws-down most precious.

"They're so small," I said. "Is it really okay to take them now?"

Sadie nodded. "They recommend up to eight weeks before weaning with the larger breeds, but Netherlands can be weaned at five. They've been on solid food for almost a week now."

They came in assorted colors: two black, one brown, one white. Sadie said the white and brown ones (Himalayan and sable) would get their markings later. We took turns cuddling them. A longing for all of them swept over me, and I dreamt of a life where baby bunnies frolicked about a Beatrix Potter thatched cottage, and around my feet, every day. As they hopped and played, performing marvelous stunts like standing on their hind legs and giving their whiskers a washin', Lily, after only a few minutes, made up her mind. She wanted a black female, just like Boopsidoodle, one of the psychedelic cartoon animals created by girls' merchandise phenomenon Lisa Frank. A few days earlier, when she showed me a small stuffed animal, the prototype for her perfect rabbit, I forewarned her that the bunnies we'd find were not likely to have outsized Kryptonite-green eyes.

I, too, wanted a female. I'd been told by the feed store owner who sold us the lop-eared that two males would not get along. Actually, her exact words were, "You don't want to get two males. Males have been known to try to castrate each other." The image of testosterone-crazed rabbits, gore dripping from furry herbivore mouths, made me decide that would never happen. A female, on the other hand, would fulfill my grander, secret scheme; I wanted the rabbits to have a litter, just one, so the girls and I could experience the wonder of mammalian pet birth.

I wondered aloud if Sadie was sure of the sexes, since baby rabbit genitalia are not exactly easy to discern. In spite of their notorious reputations, even grown rabbits can sometimes have, to put it delicately, "discreet" sex organs. Sadie laughed. "I've been doing this for a while. I have two does and a buck I breed regularly." I asked her about breeding. Obviously, this was Sadie's hobby and passion — she was the grand mistress of bunny love, priestess of pet procreation.

"It'll be about six months before the female's mature enough. You can keep them together until then; they should get along fine. But once they get together, they'll have a litter in about 30 days *to the day*."

"And how soon can she get pregnant again?"

"Almost immediately." In a hushed tone, she added that the father should be kept away from them, and the mother might eat the first litter as well.

Sadie came from rural Kansas, where her family had raised rabbits for food and pelts. As a former small-town Missourian, I could relate. The occasional wild rabbit in the frying pan, compliments of my dad's hunting skills, was a part of my youth as well. Sadie was now, like me, a city girl — she wasn't in it for food or pelts, and, at 25 dollars each, the dwarfs were pretty safe from being bought as food for city pythons.

Lily finally settled on one of the two black females, her version of Boopsie.

* * *

Lily named her brown-eyed baby Satine, after Nicole Kidman's character in *Moulin Rouge* (there is a degree of permissiveness in our household regarding letting children view bawdy and wildly romantic films). Satine and Puff got along well, though Puff tried to hump her every now and then. This caused us alarm, particularly in the beginning when Satine was one third his size, and I became angry the time or two Puff pulled out a mouthful of fur. Later, when Satine got a little older, I'm sorry to admit the humping became a source of amusement to my daughters. I'd read that this (humping, not laughing at it) was a show of dominance, also used by female rabbits on the young ones, a *Lepus* pecking order thing.

We found some large, collapsible metal pens that we could use as bunny playpens during the day. The rabbits had room to leap, sniff, hop, run, nibble grass, and stretch out on their bellies under a shrub, while we kept an eye on them. The girls played with them, pushing them around in Lily's wicker baby carriage, and they'd sometimes entertain themselves by fiddling with the bunnies' mouths, making their upper lips stick up so you could see their buck teeth. Bunny yawns caused mirth too; there was something about those huge incisors, top and bottom, and all the tiny teeth on the sides that gave the yawns a deliciously comic effect. At night we'd return them to their hutch.

A rabbit magazine I found had an article on bunny "hypnotism." We tried it. To put a rabbit in a trance, you lay it on your lap, on its back, then use both your hands to stroke the sides of its head, from front to back and up its ears. Usually, within less than a minute, the rabbit will be slack-jawed, legs straight up in the air, eyes half-opened and glassy, perfectly still. Even peals of laughter would not raise Puff, who soon became so easily hypnotized Zora could merely flip him over and he'd go under.

Then one day Zora noticed Puff "chewing" at times when he wasn't eating. I didn't pay much attention, at first, thinking the rabbity mastication motions a tic, probably something rabbits just did. A few days later I noticed a hard spot under his jaw. I wondered if it was abnormal, so I felt and compared his jaw with Satine's. I couldn't tell a difference. Scanning several books on rabbits and small farm animals led to a dead end. Andy checked him out and came to the same prognosis — there didn't seem to be cause for alarm.

A few more days passed, and it became noticeable, a definite bump, and he looked thinner. He was having trouble eating. Panic-stricken, I got a referral from our veterinarian (who didn't do bunnies) for someone who did and made an appointment

The next day the girls and I took Puff to see Dr. Jeff Dormer.

The receptionist led us into a small, white examining room, and soon Dr. Dormer breezed in. *He's young*, I thought. Dr. Dormer smiled, an earnest, boyish smile that reminded me of Doogie Houser, the teenaged TV doctor played by Neil Patrick Harris in the '80s.

*Great. Now that I'm nearing 40, I'm seeing 30-year-old doctors as young whipper-snappers.*

"And who do we have here?" he asked.

I explained Puff's situation as the girls looked on and the doctor nodded, lips pressed together, eyes solemn. He took Puff to another room to weigh him. As soon the door closed, Lily looked up at me, straightened her dress, and asked, "Do I look alright?"

This is a girl who at age three, on trips to the library, used to bring me romance paperbacks with Fabio on the cover, saying, "You should check these books out, Mommy." Now, with a mixture of horror and pride, I thought, *Oh God, she's going to be just like me, a dreamy flirt.*

Zora chortled, looking first at me, then Lily. "Gawd Lily! Lily's in luuuuve."

"Stop it, Zora," Lily said.

"Cut it out, both of you."

Dr. Dormer came back and told us Puff weighed in at just under 2 lbs. Underweight, but not alarmingly so. He put him on antibiotics for a week and scheduled surgery to open the abscess. He suggested I buy baby food to mix with the medicine.

I bought jars of spinach, peas, and carrots. When we got home, I got out the mortar and pestle to grind the pills. I let the girls be in charge of the feedings. Puff ate from a saucer; food covered his mouth and chest at each meal.

The next week we brought him in and found out he'd lost half a pound, one-quarter of his weight.

* * *

In spite of his compromised condition, Dr. Dormer decided to go ahead with the surgery, and Puff made it through. More than anything, the weight loss horrified me and filled me with guilt. I decided to take charge of all feedings. The doctor gave us an oral syringe and instructed us to give Puff three 12cc syringes of baby food or pureed vegetables six times a day, mixed with antibiotics for two of those feedings.

I fed him organic baby food mixed with milk. I ground pills, I dumped cans of mixed vegetables (carrot, potato, and green bean) in the blender and divided the portions into small plastic containers for the fridge. I warmed the food in the microwave, then I sat him in my lap, and squirted the food into his mouth, a small amount at a time, and waited for him to get it down. Each feeding took 15 minutes. Zora helped, placing hot compresses on the gaping wound and cleaning it, giving him a feeding or two each day and a bath every few days. We took turns cleaning up his diarrhea.

He was the perfect patient, docile and hungry with a strong will to live. He'd meet me at the door of the cage every time I came to feed him. Holding him for hours made me notice things about him, how his ears would cross slightly when he was concentrating on eating, how his once sort of creepy-strange pink eyes were actually quite beautiful, how his left ear was slightly longer than his right. The food got all over him, no matter how careful we were. I wanted to cry at every feeding.

After 10 days, he was looking better. I could tell he'd gained weight, yet the abscess was still huge, still big-marble-sized, and he couldn't eat any solids except hay and lettuce. I tried grinding up some of the rabbit pellets, but they went untouched.

I drove across town for more antibiotics and was told to bring in Puff again in a week. After five days and still no change, the frustration and exhaustion began to take its toll. The endless feedings, our living room as sick bay, seeing him like a furred half-ghost, the trips to the store to buy food, everything wore on me. *How long could this go on? Shouldn't there be some major change by this time?* With another round of antibiotics and another call to Dr. Dormer looming, I decided to see what I could find out about this problem on the internet. Even though I was, at the time, basically computer illiterate, it didn't take long to locate information under "Rabbit Health, Jaw Abscesses."

The first article was on face abscesses. It didn't say much about jaws, instead singling out abscesses of the teeth, a not-uncommon affliction. It described them as being extremely difficult to treat and usually a recurring problem, often requiring a *lifetime* of antibiotic treatment. The overall prognosis was guarded to poor. The article said it didn't do much good to leave any abscess open because they cannot drain like dog and cat abscesses; the pus, as Dr. Dormer told us, was too thick. My gut tightened as I began to intuit the ugly inevitable. Another article included a list of treatments, all long-term, all calling for more surgery or dangerous chemicals. The last one, called bead treatment, detailed the making and implantation of antibiotic-soaked clay pellets that would have to be made by the vet because they weren't commercially available. It was said to be "promising" but cited no actual data of failure or success.

There it was, in black and white — guarded to poor. Now I was pretty sure Puff had a tooth abscess, not a jaw abscess, and unless I devoted God-knows-how-much more money and time on a quixotic veterinary mission, he didn't stand a chance. And even if I barreled ahead, he would most likely be on antibiotics *for the rest of his life.* An invalid dwarf rabbit, requiring years of nursing care. Something I could not, would not, do, Sam I Am. Not for a bunny, not with our money. Doogie Houser looks be damned, I felt anger toward Dr. Dormer. The vet had either not known, or not leveled with me. If he had known, he should have been straight with us on the very first visit. No, it wouldn't have been pleasant to tell a woman with two apple-cheeked grammar-school girls that the prognosis for Puff was bad, that Puff had probably gnawed his last carrot. And if Doogie was clueless, too wet behind the ears to know Puff was screwed, then, goddamn it, he should have found out. *He* should have spent a little time on research, like I had. *He should have done his job.*

There were only two things left to do: share the burden of my knowledge with my husband and get a second opinion from another vet, one who was, this time, more familiar with rabbits. Becky had highly recommended her vet, Dr. Partlet, after I'd taken Puff in the first time. Now I cringed, recalling how I'd said, "No, we've already been to Dr. Dormer, and I think we should stay with him." What loyalty! What an idiot. I also remember Becky had given me her sage opinion about rabbit illnesses and mortality: "There's a reason why animals like mice and rabbits procreate so quickly. They have a lot of predators. There's a lot of things that can get them."

That afternoon I had Puff's papers faxed from Dr. Dormer's to Dr. Partlet's, and I gathered up the internet literature.

I wanted Andy's support, a confirmation of my decision, and his sympathy. That afternoon, while the girls were at a friend's house, I cornered him. I laid out all the medical information. Meekly, I fessed up to how much I'd spent on treatment.

"Almost two hundred dollars! We can't afford this!"

"It just sort of added up," I said. "Anyway, I used the money in my account, money that I had left over from last year's gardening work."

"You spent two hundred dollars on a *rabbit*?"

Now he was becoming belligerent. This wasn't just a rabbit, it was *Puff*.

"Just how," I inquired, snottily, "can you put a price on the value of a life?"

"Well," Andy deadpanned, "a bunny's limit is one hundred dollars, a cat's is two hundred dollars, and a dog's is five hundred."

I scoffed. "And what about *you*?"

"A thousand."

I couldn't help but laugh.

After a few moments of silence he asked, "How old does Satine have to be to get pregnant?"

"I've already thought about that. She's too young. She won't be able to make babies for a few more months."

"Dammit," he said. "This is what pets are about, they're a big pain in the ass."

"No, this is what life's all about, the good and the bad."

"Sandy, some people don't even make two hundred dollars in a week."

He was right. This was an incredible indulgence. There were people struggling out there to keep a roof over their heads. "But he's so sweet," I protested weakly. "It's not like he's this mean, little jerk of a bunny."

"Oh, so a life's value is determined by personality? That's fair."

I admit it, I was bicycling outside the neighborhood of Rational. Days of nursing Puff, worrying over what to do, trying to make the best decision, trying to be a good person. I couldn't keep him on antibiotics forever, or hand-feed him baby food indefinitely; in fact, I couldn't keep any of it up for much longer. I was tired. Depressed.

His life was in my hands, and I was too big a wuss to deliver the death sentence. Yet, aside from a miracle, I didn't see an alternative. I'd only faced animal euthanasia once before, with the pet chicken Suzie. Frankly, we hadn't been close. I took a deep breath. It was time to buck up. Time to be a grown-up.

"Andy, I'm taking him in tomorrow, one last time. If he can't be cured, I'll have him put to sleep."

After Andy left, I sat down and cried. Then I wondered: *Had Puff's life really had any quality these last few weeks?* If he'd been in the wild, he'd be gone already, long gone. Suddenly I realized something else about this free bunny; maybe his previous owner had faced this same decision. She, too, could have nursed him through an abscess, then decided to quietly pass him on. She could have rationalized it by thinking, well, maybe he won't get sick again. *That's why he was free!* I thought. *Make him someone else's problem, give him away.* At that moment I despised her and Doogie Houser equally. Then I did something even more difficult; I thought about my role. *Who was I really doing all this for? Were these extreme measures for Puff, or for me?* With no little pain, I began to realize my biggest investment in this drama had been my opinion of myself. Yes, it was the same ole story, all about me, me, me.

Zora and Lily came home from their friends' house and found me in the living room, sitting on the chair near Puff's cage, puff-y eyed.

Zora walked over to me. "Mom, you look upset." She laid a hand on my shoulder.

I found myself tearing up again, explaining to my girls what was happening, what I'd learned on the internet. I told them I was worried that this was it, the end of the bunny trail for Puff. That I'd made another appointment for tomorrow, just to be sure.

"I love Puff," Zora said, "but you can't spend all your time trying to fix him."

* * *

The stucco office building, decorated in a southwestern motif, held the practice of three vets. Lily busied herself looking at animal health brochures with cute pictures of puppies and kittens, while Zora sat with Puff in his wooden cage on her lap. I dug into a stack of paperwork, more than most multi-thousand-dollar contracts require.

Lily stayed behind when one of Dr. Partlet's assistants came for us. The assistant reminded me of Satine's breeder, Sadie. They had the same Midwestern accent, wholesome demeanor, and plump corn-fed look. When I asked her if she was from Colorado, she smiled. "No, my family's from Kansas." Once we were in the examining room, she took Puff out to be weighed.

Dr. Partlet, an attractive forty-something woman with a trim figure and shoulder length blonde hair, brought Puff back in. Her assistant followed.

"He's gained back six ounces," she said, smiling.

Although she said she'd perused the other vet's paperwork, she asked the same questions: How long has he been sick? What has been done? What are you doing now? She began to examine him, bypassing his abscess and looking directly into his mouth. Immediately she pointed out dense milk-colored pus, coming up from his gumline at his bottom incisors. My heart fell.

"That's pus?" Zora said. "I thought that was plaque, I've been scraping it off."

"She knows what plaque is?" asked the assistant. "That's pretty impressive for a girl her age."

Dr. Partlet agreed, and they both smiled at my 10-year-old daughter in a way that suggested: "Maybe one day she'll be one of us." My feeling of pride was diminished by nausea at the thought of Zora "scraping it off."

The doctor told us she was sure that the abscess came from the bottom incisors. She said she could go back in surgically and try to take out more of the infected tissue, while continuing antibiotic treatment, but eventually the teeth would have to come out. She explained about teeth trimming (which would become necessary) and feeding, all in an optimistic we-can-do-this tone. My head swam.

I couldn't believe she seemed enthusiastic about starting treatment, as if this were just a rousing challenge.

I interrupted her. "But even if we did all this, there's still no guarantee that it would solve the problem?"

"No, not really," said the doctor.

"Or that there wouldn't be recurring abscesses?"

"Yes, it's possible it could recur."

"Not to mention the feeding difficulties we'll have," I said.

My dam of information broke. I told the doctor what I had read about abscesses, the general prognosis of "guarded to poor," and told her that while we loved Puff, I couldn't see how we could justify doing more surgery. My eyes filled with tears. In the face of the doctor's optimism, I was carrying out the death sentence. I had told Andy the night before that putting a cute little bunny to sleep, even one as messed up as Puff, seemed somehow sinful.

The vet nodded in agreement to everything I said. After finishing, I stood there trying to compose myself. Dr. Partlet waited patiently, sympathetically. Finally, I asked, "Can you do it?"

"Yes." She asked if we wanted to be present. I didn't, but Zora said she did.

The doctor looked at me. "If she wants to be here," I said, "it's her choice."

"I do," said Zora.

"I'll stay then, too."

I looked at my daughter. *Where did she get this courage?* Certainly not from me. My insides felt like jelly, and my head was light. Even though I had been through natural childbirth, twice, I actually worried that I might swoon. The doctor and her assistant left to get another form and the lethal shot.

"Zora, are you sure you want to be here?"

"Yes, Mom."

I stood weak-kneed by my girl.

They came back, and I signed the paperwork for the euthanasia. The assistant put a box of tissues on top of Puff's wood transport cage, "just in case."

I grabbed one and began dabbing the flow.

The veterinarian looked at Puff's ears, first swabbing them with alcohol.

"I don't see a vein that's going to be big enough. These guys are so tiny. Our other option is to inject the abdomen. It takes longer for the drug to work that way, but I don't think we'll have a choice."

"He won't feel pain, will he?" I asked. I knew the answer, knew how the drug paralyzed the muscles, the nervous system, finally the respiratory and circulatory systems. And we couldn't really ask them how it feels, now, could we?

"No, but it might take up to a half hour. First, he will lie down, but it may take a while for the heart to completely stop." She went into the details, how to feel his heart. I knew about his heart, I'd felt it beat many times as I held him. I'd even noticed his breathing after we'd picked him up after surgery. His nose had moved so slowly, yet still looked so cute; I noted this even as I wondered if he'd die from the stress.

I felt sorry for the veterinarian. How many beloved family members had she had to put down? Maybe she had seemed ready to go to extreme measures to save Puff because that was her training — what society — expected from her. And maybe it wasn't the veterinarians who were supposed to have the guts to make the difficult decisions; maybe it was us.

I turned away, tears flowing. She injected him. Zora looked on, then patted Puff reassuringly.

They put him back in the wooden case. He was paralyzed, limp, eyes open.

I went outside to the waiting room, tissues in hand, nose running, and paid the bill. Lily had done well waiting for us, but now she looked at me and I could see her worry, over *me*. We got into the car for the ten-block trip home. Zora sat up front.

"Can I take him out of the cage?" she asked.

Inside, I thought, *Oh no, please don't,* but I said, "I don't know, Zora. . . . When he goes, well, he might make a mess."

"I don't care."

"Well, okay then."

She held him on her lap, stroking him.

I pulled up in our driveway, with two little girls and a dying bunny.

"He's gone," Zora said.

I looked across at her. She was teary but holding it together. Only I was at the ragged edge of despair, sobbing. Puff's beautiful candy pink eyes were clouded, dull. He was gone. We got out of the car and went into the house to grieve, to think on lessons gleaned from our Lilliputian, ill-fated friend. We'd have the funeral later, when Andy came home.

# Please Don't Piss on the Petunias

There he lay, in the middle of the backyard, in one of the few spots he hadn't either left his mark on or attempted to destroy. On his back — big, black, and furry — splayed legs up in the air, head to one side, mouth slack and slightly open, eyes closed. The morning sun shone on his wantonly exposed, impressively large, canine private parts.

*He looks dead*, I thought as I sipped my coffee and stared out the window of the back door. I smiled. *Dare I hope?*

As if my thought had somehow reached him telepathically, he stirred, then got up and shook. *Damn,* I thought, *the beast lives.*

I didn't hate the black Lab, and I didn't really wish him dead, though at the time he was the bane of my existence. I hated his owner, Andy.

\* \* \*

It began at the flea market, on a Saturday morning at the end of July. Our family had split off in two directions as we often do, yin and yang, me with Zora and Lily, Andy off on his own. The females would indulge in girlie stuff, toys and books, while Andy searched for tools and other manly items. Normally, we met up again near the end, so I was surprised when he found us midway through the rows.

"There's something I want to show you," he told us. "Someone has some black Lab pups."

"Puppies? I thought they weren't allowed to sell them here anymore."

He shrugged, and then said impatiently, "Come on."

Of course, the girls were thrilled. As we walked, in a hurry, lest the puppies get snatched up, I noticed Andy's slightly maniacal smile, the excited gleam in his eyes. He asked me, "Do you think I should get one?"

"I don't know," I said, in a tone that I hoped revealed my reluctance.

Andy led us to a space next to a big white pickup truck, where a male pup and his sister bounced around in a wire pen half covered with a towel for shade. The sellers, two freckle-faced teenagers, a well-mannered brother and sister, explained that their family, in the dog breeding business, was moving to Texas. The asking price on the AKC-registered, three-month-old pups was bargain-basement low. They had even had their first shots and a deworming. They looked sleek and beautiful, very happy. The girls squealed, and each picked one up.

Andy got caught up in the moment. To him, it must have seemed almost predestined. It was a week before his birthday, and we'd found our first dog, Cato, also a black Lab, at the flea market more than fourteen years earlier. Cato had died the previous summer. Over the year had Andy mentioned he wanted another Lab, but I hadn't taken him seriously because we already had a dog, three-year-old Alice, a Dalmatian rescued from the Humane Society. Andy hadn't been for getting Alice at all, but Zora and I fell in love with the five-month-old spotted beauty. Zora cried for her, I made my case, and Andy caved in.

Now I realized Alice had never been his idea of the ideal dog. Andy knew only collies, retrievers, and Labs from his childhood. Alice was a spotted strangeling — thrilling to me but out of his comfort zone. I remembered how on the first week we had her he related second-hand horror stories about Dalmatian temperament, and at one point enlightened me on another Dalmatian factoid. "My sister says they're a gay man's dog. She told me Gene Simmons has a bunch of them."

I laughed out loud, imagining the lead singer of Kiss (a notorious horn-dog) surrounded by the "gay man's dog." I corrected him, "I think you mean *Richard* Simmons." I had looked over at Alice, who happened to be lounging on our cabbage rose-print sofa. The black and white contrast, pattern against pattern, was *stunning. Why, of course,* I thought, my own sense of taste bolstered by the revelation, *that makes sense. Dalmatians are such a feast for the eyes, exquisite.*

Black Labs, on the other hand, were not fancy polka dot dogs. As we stood gazing upon the hounds, I remembered the comments he'd made over the last year about Labradors' attributes: loyalty, gentleness, intelligence, obedience. Still, I'd pooh-poohed the idea of a second dog, a second *big* dog. It was obvious to me one was plenty; we had our replacement, we'd gone almost a whole year as a one-dog family again, and life was simpler. Less dog poop. A good thing.

As Andy bent to pick up the male pup for a third time, a feeling of big trouble washed over me. I felt like stepping in, announcing (like a man whose wife wants to have yet another baby), "Whaddaya wanna go and do that for? Ain't life good as it is?" I didn't see this as providence; I saw it as a potential pain in the ass — my ass. I was the one who cleaned up after the dogs. But I made my mistake; I held my tongue.

Instead of saying, "No, please no, God no, this is a bad idea, I'll do anything if you walk away right now!" I declared in a self-righteous tone that I would not stand in the way of his personal pet happiness. Translation: *"Even though you've tried to stifle me at times, I, the much superior human being, will not do the same to you."* Then I made it clear I would not be part of the puppy project. I think my exact, whispered words were, *"You* have to take care of him. I will *not.* I have enough to deal with." The memories of Alice's puppydom, four-pawed hell, OCD-style gnawing, and uncontrolled bodily functions, were still vivid.

Andy, in turn, reminded me to curb my bitchery. He declared puppy love his right as the girls and I had more than our fair share of animal indulgences. And didn't have to remind me how our household was lopsided in the male/female ratio — me, our girls, *and* the dog. The canary was male, and so were two of the chickens, but that hardly mattered. Andy was outnumbered. He knew it, and I knew it. My sense of fairness won. As he cradled the pup, I pled guilty as charged but reminded him again that I took care of mine, and I expected the same from him.

Andy wrote a check, and we bounded, floppy-eared, into insanity.

\* \* \*

Three days later, the morning my sister was due to arrive with her three sons for a 10-day visit, I awoke to find two piles of puppy poop and two puddles of puppy pee in the house.

"Oh, Andy!" I yelled for, already, the umpteenth time. He cleaned it up, always, but I always had to point it out.

\* \* \*

The next week, with five children running around — twin six-year-old boys, Cody and Cory (born on the same day as Lily), their twelve-year-old brother, Christopher, and our girls — proved so chaotic that the puppy blended right in. He was played with, toted about, and transferred to the back porch, where he could go outside on his own to do his business. He liked it there, didn't mind sleeping alone. Quite the independent fellow.

The biggest problem we had at that point was thinking of a name.

During the visit, the boys convinced my girls the puppy should be named after Darth Vader. They began calling him Darth, and I was forced to make a stand. I told them that although I hadn't exactly welcomed the pup with open arms, he would not be named after an evil space villain. I suggested Ewan instead, after the dishy Scottish actor who played Obi Wan Kenobi. They hooted at that. Andy thought of the name Buddy, and I pretended to gag. Victoria suggested Cyrus, with a nickname of Cy, but that wasn't quite right either — too dignified. We looked at the pup's papers for ideas and discovered his mother was a black Lab and his father a yellow Lab. Names on the paternal side included Joker's Wild I through VI, and names on the maternal side included a shock — the pup's granddad was named Sampson's Shining Sambo. *How sad*, I thought, *the owners' choices of names indicate probable gamblers and racists.*

Andy had named our previous Lab, Cato, and like a well-respected ancient Roman statesman, he showed qualities of wisdom, dignity, and superior intelligence. This dog was no Cato. He was bigger, bouncier, goofier, and somehow more laid back. I suspected he was lacking in intelligence, but it was hard to tell. He reminded me of a stoned surfer dude.

My sister's visit ended with the dog still unnamed, and the focus shifted to training. Without five children playing outside much of the day, and with Andy at work, the dog was now left mostly on his own, under my neglect. I reminded Andy it was time to start taking his dog to work, like he'd said he planned to do when we got him. Andy demurred. Things began to get ugly.

"But I thought he was going to be your work dog!" I said.

"I can't take him this week."

"No problem, but I'm not training him, Andy. He can stay outside."

Andy took him to get his shots and license. On the third week, I made the comment that perhaps we should call him Vietnamese Pot Belly Pig as his stomach was quite roly-poly. He had worms. Andy made another trip to the vet and began the deworming process for both dogs. Everyone, especially Andy, grossed out, and barefoot-in-the-gardenness was banned.

Alice tolerated the puppy but made it clear to him that the house was her domain. She snarled and snapped if he tried to enter without her permission. That was okay with me, as long as he wasn't parasite-free and potty-trained. I did bring him in briefly each morning, to fetch the paper — a trick I taught him, which, with a retriever, is about as difficult as teaching a canary to sing. He'd bring the paper to Andy, who was invariably still in bed. Andy had taught Cato many things — fetch (including "get the duct tape"), speak, sit, roll over, and even "put it in the trash," to pick up litter — but he didn't seem interested in getting up and teaching this one anything.

We finally named him, settling on a name I'd thought of, after an old blues musician, Big Bill Broonzy. Andy and I had learned about

Broonzy when we had taken an American Jazz class together in college. I thought the name had playfulness and machismo. Andy liked it. The kids didn't, but since they weren't cleaning up after him (I was, more and more), they had no vote.

I had been hoping the puppy would help with Andy's depression, an ongoing part of our lives since the loss of his brother, five years before, and his mother, a year later. I could understand grief, but not Andy's never-ending abyss.

I wanted it to be over. I was dead sick of the sorrow. We had so much to be grateful for, so many blessings: happy, healthy, children; our health (physical, at least); a lovely home. I watched in awe as our children grew before my eyes, while their father, in his dark cloud, seemed to miss so many things. Andy had his own timetable; I couldn't change it. No one could. I felt resentment and hurt — a hurt that came out too often as anger. And now I saw that even a cute puppy dog didn't stand a chance of breaking through the gloom.

Maybe I could have tried to find out how to deal with the situation in a healthier way, but I didn't. I was unaware, I was too busy, we didn't have the money for therapy. Instead, I reminded Andy on a daily basis of his responsibility to his dog.

"He's too young to take to work," my husband said each time I brought up the work-dog subject. "He could get hurt."

He, in turn, reminded me that I didn't have a paying job, that I was indulging myself "trying" to be a writer and staying home with the children and animals. Oh, and the gardening was a financial pain in *his* ass.

Weeks passed.

Andy didn't keep Broonzy in rawhides for teething, as I had with Alice, and although we all gave him some attention, it wasn't nearly enough. So, over the rest of the summer and early fall, Broonzy entertained himself and eased his teething discomfort by systematically destroying everything he could get his mouth on in my most beloved of spaces, my garden. Eight cushions on four metal garden chairs (chairs that I'd bought secondhand and carefully restored) torn up and dispersed into bits; two adorable wooden children's chairs reduced to splinters; pots broken; plants pawed from the ground. A tiny clematis I'd just spent weeks nurturing disappeared one day. Nothing left but a hole. *Broonzy.* I would scream and sometimes sob after finding each new destruction: structures despoiled, beans bitten, sunflowers savaged, petunias pissed on. When Andy got home, my howling could probably be heard halfway down the block.

Andy would apologize, sometimes remind me again to get a job, and then do nothing. Well, to be fair, he'd spend a little extra time with the beast, throwing a ball around for a while, but by the next day things would be back to abnormal. My personality, normally more on the easygoing side, didn't help — I'd go from bitch to Buddha, over and over and over again. I hated the situation and didn't like myself much either.

Six weeks into Broonzy's life with us, and after another backyard fight prompted by a random act of puppy violence, Andy made a confession. "I shouldn't have gotten him. I admit it."

I knew he felt this way, but now he actually admitted it. This was a breakthrough. I softened. *Poor Andy, poor Broonzy, poor me.* I also felt sorry for our children, who had to witness their nut-case parents' antics.

"Well then," I suggested, "why don't we just find him a new home? We could find him a good one. I read that Labs are the most popular breed."

"I can't."

"What do you mean, you can't?" I said, looking around the yard at the chewed-up plastic sprinkler, the headless Beanie Baby bear near the back steps, and the strewn bits of fluff from a destroyed cushion sticking to some of the remaining greenery.

"I don't think it's right. If you commit to getting an animal, you should stick with it."

"Oh God, Andy! I know we've never gotten rid of an animal, but this is different! I'll tell you what — what if *I* can find someone who wants him? You won't even have to be involved."

"I wouldn't feel right about it."

After 18 years, you know someone pretty well. Without Andy's consent, I would not take action, and he would not consent. We stayed stuck on the hamster wheel of insanity.

I thought of how Alice's puppyhood had lasted until she was two and didn't see how I could possibly hang in there that long. I vacillated between crazed screaming of empty threats, a grudging tolerance, and patting the little shit on the head now and then. (Broonzy, not Andy — well, sometimes Andy.)

Over the next months, the list of destroyed articles grew. He chewed off the corner of our picnic table, knocked over more planters and scattered their contents, ate a wooden chair on the back porch, along with a large wicker basket, and ravished a small bookcase I'd primed, painted, and stupidly left outside for an hour (unguarded) to dry. Broonzy dragged out the water lilies from our pond and gnawed on their thick tuberous roots. I'd catch him, yell and berate him, and replant the lilies, only to find them retriever-ed again a day later. He destroyed the five-foot-by-eight-foot pond by wading into it and poking holes in the liner with his claws. All but two of the fish had died before I made this discovery. As I ran into the house to get a container for the two survivors, he ate one of them. I gnashed my teeth, pulled my hair, and begged God to *please let him run away*.

He did take off once but to my great disappointment was returned. The good Samaritan made a comment about what a "nice" dog I had. I joked about giving the dog to him, all the while searching the stranger's face for a clue, any clue, that it could be a possibility. I heard from an old friend about a couple whose marriage had disintegrated, the last straw being a black Lab puppy. The story rang heartbreakingly true. I sobbed, claiming this dog was killing me and killing our marriage.

But I knew Broonzy was a scapegoat. I wasn't really dying, and we were killing our own marriage.

The dysfunction continued. To keep my spirits up, I occasionally made fun of the dog, who looked quite freaky for a while. At five months he had stubby legs, a big barrel body, and an enormous head.

I wondered, with a sort of macabre fascination, if his legs would ever catch up. *Maybe he would grow up to look as hideous as his deeds*, I mused. It was almost disappointing when he stopped looking so weird. His legs finally lengthened, but still he did not resemble our other lab, the good one, who had been, of course, beautifully formed — not too large, not too small, just right. Broonzy was becoming, in contrast, a square-headed behemoth. One afternoon a male friend who'd stopped by remarked on the dog's "block-headed handsomeness." *You must be kidding!* I thought. *He's ugly!* After the friend left, I stepped back and tried to see Broonzy through male eyes. *Why, of course. He's machismo incarnate; a big, brutish, testosterone-fueled tank; a tank systematically mowing down my loving, nurturing existence. What wasn't to admire?*

Yet somehow the dog could sense that my oft-hateful vibes were not pure. He radiated puppy love, and he loved me, like he loved everyone and everything else. Whenever I gardened, or fed the chickens, he was right behind me, his eyes darting up at my face submissively, his mouth open in that slack, slobbery smile, trying to get in my good graces, which was impossible. Sometimes he would nip me on the backside with his tiny front teeth — I would yell out (it really hurt), and he would get an expression of amusement, which amused me. I would scold him, and then pet him. I had given up on Andy taking him during the day, and my resentment simmered. Though I offered to give him away to everyone I knew (Broonzy, not Andy — well, sometimes Andy), there were no takers.

In the fall, just when we'd begun to settle into our dysfunctional setup of destruction, screaming, resentment, and grudging tolerance, just when I thought it couldn't get worse, it did. The telephone rang one day, and our next-door neighbor Paul alerted me, "Linda just looked out the bedroom window and your puppy's out there rousting about with one of the chickens."

*Rousting about? Oh, shit!*

"I'll be right out!"

I dropped the phone and ran. Broonzy lay near the lilac bush with Kayley in his mouth like a chew toy. White feathers were scattered about. "You son of a . . ." I screamed.

Broonzy stood up and sauntered away from the chicken, who was lying very still, eyes closed.

While I raved, at the same time checking for injuries to the bird (Kayley was okay, so to speak; he'd been playing a form of chicken-opossum), Broonzy gave me his infamous Duhhh-did-I-do-something-wrong? look. He dared to stand close by, blinking at me with slightly slanted, dark amber eyes. *My God*, I thought, *he's grown huge — a big, nasty brute!* His insistent bad behavior felt like my husband's oppressive unhappiness, having its way with us. My rage grew.

The plant and property destruction I could cope with, but now he'd crossed the line, picking on a little bird. My inner barbarian took over, and a switch on the ground caught my eye. I grabbed it, grabbed the culprit and gave him a half-dozen lashes on his rump whilst shrieking like a wild woman: "No! No! No!" I knew I was probably being watched by the neighbors, but I cared not one bit what they thought.

After the scene, Broonzy only walked away, wagging his tail, as if he had no concept whatsoever of the magnitude of the event, as if he hadn't felt the switching, as if he were mocking me. My sympathies were for the chicken, but my guilt was worse. Not only for my brutish behavior toward the dog but also for my gutless unwillingness to find him a new home and my stubborn refusal to train him. I was equally at fault for the chicken's suffering. I was partially at fault for Broonzy's behavior.

Andy came home that evening to a fresh hell of a brand-new flavor. Before he even had his hand on the doorknob, I was there.

"This is *it*! You have to do something!"

"What do you want me to do?" he asked after I unleashed the tale. "They're bred to retrieve birds."

I could not believe my ears. A slew of obscenities burst forth, ending with, ". . . Cato didn't mess with the chickens!"

"Oh, yes he did."

"Oh no he didn't! I was here!"

Perfect rational maturity. It didn't matter. Incredibly enough, by this time, a part of me had become oddly, sickeningly, resolved to the fact we'd never get rid of him. "Well, if Alice can learn, so can he," I said. Alice, who had accidentally injured a chicken when she was a puppy, had reacted to my horrific display of yelling with obedience. She never touched a chicken again.

But Broonzy was no Alice.

Andy tried to console me with the fact he didn't think Broonzy would hurt the chickens because retrievers are "soft mouthed," meaning they were bred to retrieve birds without mutilating them. I'd heard the same, but that didn't set my heart at ease.

I told Andy I would not lock up the half dozen free-ranging chickens because that would teach Broonzy nothing. Instead, I resolved to take it upon myself, in this alone, to be vigilant — I would watch the dog and guard the chickens. Surely, I thought, the dog could learn. Surely, he was not a total bonehead. *Maybe*, the hopeful thought entered my mind, *he'd already learned his lesson and wouldn't do it again.*

Ah, the naiveté! The first incident proved to be just that, in a two-week-long celebration of chicken torture. Several days later I caught Broonzy dragging our rooster Jane, the Silkie, across the yard. One of Jane's wings was extended in a particularly pathetic way, as if he were trying to slow his abduction. I switched Broonzy again, yelled and screamed again, revealed my inner bitch, my inner lunatic. Once more, Broonzy reacted with nonchalance. Though Jane seemed uninjured, a few days later he died.

I upped the surveillance, keeping an eye on the backyard hourly. The bitch alarm sounded every time Broonzy went near a chicken, every time he even looked at one. Then, after a few days break in activity, another incident. I found another circular area of white feathers in the lawn and Kayley in the chicken coop, buried face down in the pine shaving litter. I was sure he was dead this time; he looked headless. The tiny golden Silkie hen, Flora, who weighed two pounds at the most (an addition to the flock that spring) was in the henhouse too, next to him, guarding the body. *Brave little one,* I thought, *putting yourself in a vulnerable position for Broonzy's attention.* Steadying myself for the worst, I pulled the bird out. His head was attached. *Hallelujah, he lived!* Underbelly plucked naked, half-smothered, traumatized, but alive.

This time I cried — uncle. Broonzy won. The chickens, (especially Kayley, a sweet little rooster with short feathered legs who had little chance of evading capture), were too big a temptation in the dog's too often-alone life. If he stopped, it would be of his own accord. From then on, I closed the chicken area's gate and latched it. I had to detach; I could not invest anymore time or emotion. The four chickens who could fly over the four-foot fence could take their chances.

Though his habitat area had diminished greatly, bare-breasted Kayley, amazingly hardy, once again survived the assault, and the remaining poultry wound up evading Broonzy successfully.

A week or two after this episode, I found more feathers in the yard. My heart thudded; I felt nauseated, dizzy. I was positive it was another casualty. How Broonzy reached the feather duster, hanging on the wall near the kitchen sink, I still do not know, but I was glad to be able to laugh for a change, even if it was a pained, hollow laugh.

On another day, I looked out the bathroom window onto the backyard and admired my perennial beds dusted with the season's very first snow fall. The sight always reminded me of snow globes and treats sprinkled with powdered sugar. The only aspect marring the picture was Broonzy, on the lawn, vigorously humping the blanket he'd dragged outside from his sleeping spot on the enclosed back porch.

Another evening I woke in the middle of the night to the sounds of an outside ruckus. *Oh no, Broonzy's at it again.* I strained to hear more, debating for a minute whether to get up or not. Andy, lying next to me, seemed to be fast asleep. *To hell with it,* I decided and closed my eyes, pulling the cover over my head. The next morning the racket was still going, and this time I dashed outdoors, only to find Broonzy staggering around, his head enclosed in a one-gallon poultry-water reservoir. A space dog. The thought of the unpleasant night he must have had brought an evil smile to my lips.

For Christmas the girls got Bertie Bott's Every Flavor Beans, a treat inspired by the fictional candy in the Harry Potter stories. The beans, like their namesakes, are every flavor, including revolting ones. Zora and Lily thought it would be funny to feed Alice a booger-flavored bean. She took it in her mouth, then, that's my clever girl, let it drop out. That evening they left all the yucky ones on the coffee table and Broonzy, who was allowed in the house on freezing nights, wolfed them down — booger, sardine, horseradish, and black pepper.

During this period, I had softened enough to consider sending in Broonzy's AKC registration papers and the 20-dollar fee. Registering him would be a token of good will, a Christmas present to my husband. Several times during the year I'd thought of doing it, and in December I got so far as to fill out the form. But even with the benevolent Christmas spirit filling me, I found I just could not do it.

I couldn't do it because the destruction continued. Shortly after I nixed sending the form, Broonzy destroyed Lily's new Mary Kate Olsen doll. I found her on the sofa, arms and one foot chewed to stubs, a puncture hole on her head — a maimed testimony to the brutal male force in residence. The sight of the once perfect, now horrific, doll temporarily rekindled my cause for relocating the vandal and inflamed my marital feelings of resentment, pain, and betrayal. I begged that day to get rid of him.

Seven-year-old Lily, the actual victim, played it cool. She told Andy, "Dad, you'll have to buy me another one. I earned the money for that doll, and Broonzy's your responsibility."

I admired her. Where had she learned to be reasonable? Certainly not from her parents.

Both daughters considered Broonzy a bona fide family member and even championed him. "Aww, he's a good dog," they'd say. "Isn't he cute?" they'd coo.

I could only tally the damage, which continued to grow. Perhaps in gratitude for being let in on blustery nights, he had chewed an upholstered chair arm, the handle of a beaded purse, and a leather shoe. Flea market bargain indeed; I wept to think of the emotional costs, shuddered to think of the financial.

A brand new year but the same old story.

Then spring came, along with realizations. The dog was pretty firmly entrenched; I could not count on a happy departure. It seemed that sticking with it would be the name of the game, kind of like in our marriage. As far as the garden went, we decided it would be foolish to replace the pond liner; Broonzy was still young and the pond should be redesigned to be dog proof anyway. On the positive side, my hardy water lilies had survived Broonzy's gnawing and the bitter winter. They were coming back to life in their stopgap home, the old cast iron bathtub. Even the sole surviving goldfish had made it through. Though puppyhood wasn't over, it seemed the peak of mayhem had passed.

Around his first birthday, at the end of April (it so perfectly figured that Broonzy was a bullish Taurus, like my dad), I even found myself warming up to the creature. One day, much to my delight, it occurred to me what he resembled most — a gargoyle (but with smaller nostrils). A rather friendly gargoyle. Though his presence didn't distress me as much, I hadn't entirely given up my dream of someone taking him away, far away. And I didn't stop offering.

On one particularly lovely spring day, a potential sucker came to visit. Becky, Earth mother, nature lover extraordinaire, came to see the garden. One moment we were enjoying perfect serenity, walking, chatting, checking out proliferations of buds and flowers, delighting in the renewal of it all, and in the next, both dogs barreled our way, scrambling about us in a mad play fight. Alice barked, head down, Dalmatian ass in the air, teeth bared, while Broonzy bounce-danced around her in delight. She'd race towards him and jump, he'd bound away, then he'd do the same to her. They chased each other around, weaving in and out, back and forth in front of us, woofing and arfing.

"Quiet!" I scolded, "Stop it, Alice!"

From across the gnawed picnic table, Becky said, in her soft, sensual voice, a voice you'd imagine a phone-sex solicitor would have, "It's okay, he's enjoying it. They're just playing."

"But they're so *loud*."

"It doesn't bother me, really."

I could tell by the way Becky watched them, she wasn't annoyed. Alice continued to raise hell. They barked, circled, leapt, going at it at full canine force. Alice acted as if she'd relish getting Broonzy by the throat.

The smile hadn't left Becky's face. "They're having a great time."

"But look how aggressive she's acting!"

"Oh, he can handle himself, and he knows it. Broonzy's a lot bigger and stronger than she is." Becky's statement opened my eyes. While I loathed all that virile male-dog energy, she was actually admiring it. We watched as Broonzy played the submissive, or should I say, the passive-aggressive one. Somehow the two of them reminded me of . . .

Becky, too, had admired Broonzy's good looks, and when I'd offered to give him to her the year before she said she was very tempted. Now I offered again.

"If I didn't have my two old girls at home . . ." she began, referring to her rescued dogs, "but then again, no, I don't think I would, after all. You should keep him. You know, he's going to be a great dog. I can tell."

"You can?"

"Oh, yes. He'd be great on a camping trip. Very protective."

I guffawed. "No way. He'd probably run the other way if there was ever any danger!"

"You'd be surprised. I think you underestimate him, Sandy."

I knew Becky was in tune to the wild, to nature, more than any other person I'd ever met. And she adored men. She admired that maddening male energy, an irresistible energy that I had been fighting too often, for too long. Her comments softened me even further, though I couldn't resist asking if she had any ideas for a good home.

"My son has a female lab," she said. "He'd probably love to have him. I'll ask."

Later that day she called me; her son couldn't take him. I found I was not disappointed.

\* \* \*

The seasons changed again. We made it through another summer and another Christmas. It was close to Broonzy's second birthday. He'd mellowed considerably. In the last two months, he'd only eaten the contents of two cans of goldfish food (the first I left by the pond and the other he grabbed off the back porch shelf, apparently unable to resist seconds) and ravaged a few household items. He'd even become discerning; although he found fish flakes palatable, he recently refused Bertie Bott's latest jellybean flavors, vomit and dirt.

One day he jumped up on Andy's workshop table, grabbed a plastic bowl of sunflower seeds, took them outside and ate them, shells and all. A window was open, and I heard Andy yelling, so I looked outside. Andy smiled as he reproached the dog, in typical half-assed form.

"Good training, Andy," I said when he told me the story. I felt happy that Andy was smiling. I was too.

I found I no longer hated my husband. Like the pup mellowing into doghood, our relationship mayhem had also, finally, mercifully, mellowed. The saying about time and wounds held true. Yes, I was aware we could benefit from therapy, but we couldn't afford it, and it didn't matter much anyway. We were in it for the long haul, for better, for worse, for forever dysfunctional. We'd weathered this storm and others, and we'd weather more.

Andy said that in spite of it all, he didn't regret getting Broonzy. My mouth dropped open at that one. I longed to feel the same way. I daydreamed about being old together and reminiscing about that wild, but actually quite wonderful, block-headed dog we had for a very, very long time.

I thought, *I might even send in that damn registration form — one of these days.*

# Romancing the Seed

Winter. Once again, it was seed buying time, planning time, dreaming time. On a frosty Colorado Saturday morn, as I sat at the kitchen table and browsed my favorite catalogs, my thoughts turned to vegetables . . . and love. I mused at how, in spring, all the garden became a stage for romance. Pregnant buds, after a wintertime of slow hidden growth, opened joyously, revealed perfect leaves and flowers. Birds sang throaty songs of mating, and bees began their explorations, helping flowers meet.

In the catalog I saw asparagus, springtime sex incarnate as they pushed through the earth as thin chartreuse phalluses. *'Precoce d'Argenteuil'* from an Italian supplier sounded especially intriguing. In the photo, it was handsome — rosy purple with only a bit of green at the head.

Another variety, 'Purple Passion,' caught my eye — deep burgundy men with a higher sugar content than their green counterparts. Although they turned green upon cooking, I learned that sweet young spears were often savored raw — and purple. That's how I imagined eating them, raw, and in the proper way, with the fingers.

Another page offered peas. Of all the springtime blossoms, the darling peas were probably the most delicate, the most like miniature Georgia O'Keeffe masterpieces. Paradoxically, the catalog boasted varieties with male names — mighty English peas named 'Green Arrow,' 'Mr. Big,' and 'Knight.' I wondered if they were macho, after all, but then I thought of the babies, the peas in the pods. I take a deep breath, close my eyes, and my mind wanders. . . .

Peas . . . seeds . . . Suddenly I'm transported to my sun-filled potting shed, basking in the March warmth. I roll up my sleeves, ready myself for a few hours of planting. Then, just as I begin to work, Andy surprises me with a visit. I'm so pleased by his offer to help. We toil side by side, enjoying the musky smell of soil going into pots, the tepid water we spill, and the warm sunshine that envelopes us. Birds twitter and cavort in rapturous mating rituals. They are happy spring is coming. We are happy, too. Andy says I look beautiful even though my face is smudged with dirt and my hair is unloosed from its kerchief. As our fingers caress and count seeds, as we push them deep into the damp soil, the room heats up.

Simultaneously, we reach for the watering can. The touch of fingers on fingers is sweetly electric, spring-fevery. The potting shed door closes, and . . .

The daydream evaporated as Andy walked into the kitchen and saw me with the catalog. He noticed my daydreamy smile. "Try not to overspend on seeds this year," he said, "like you always do."

"Whatever," I said. My springtime fantasy faded like a pressed flower.

Winter rushed back, along with the reality of no potting shed. My seedlings would struggle in the chilly, unfinished basement, below shelves of fluorescent lights and surrounded by dust and cobwebs.

I turned the page. Eggplants. New this year was 'Slim Jim.' 'Slim Jim' was supposed to be exceptionally early, garden flower pretty, long, slender, purple, and mild. Maybe I'd enjoy their sensual flavor in a favorite Italian dish, *Pollo con le Melanzane e I Pomodori Freshi* (fricasseed chicken with eggplant and fresh tomatoes). *Delicioso*. The name 'Slim Jim' drew me back to the fantasy of spring. . . . I envisioned another Italian dish, a slender gentleman named Giacomo — dark, very sexy, and a master of culinary delights (among other things). I was sure this Jim would not try to limit the household spending, certainly not on tomatoes, perhaps the most female fruit. My catalog offered an incredible selection, but none were enticingly named. 'Green Zebra' and 'Grandma Mary' weren't very lip-smacking. I was old enough to know that a tomato used to be a word for a sexy young thing, like Betty Boop or Bettie Page. It made sense if you thought about it, the tight skin covering firm flesh, the succulent and juicy insides.

While the taste of tomatoes was not overtly sexual, they had their moments, in Italian food with wine, of course, or eaten warm off the vine, the juice dripping down one's arm. And I was sure I wasn't the only one to enjoy the sensual pleasure of pressing a cherry tomato against the roof of my mouth — and squishing it. *I should develop my own tomato*, I thought. *I would name it 'Betty.'*

Next I browsed the beans. At first, I found little in the sexiness department, few provocative names. I didn't understand why — beans are energetic, forceful — they rambled up fences and trellises, twined, curled, and grasped like possessive lovers. Then a lusty Italian pole bean, *'Purple Trionfo Violetto,'* caught my eye. This bean's vines were reported to overrun trellises, and the ornamental light-purple blooms were said to become thousands of dark purple beans, whose "nutty sweet flavor" was "just sublime."

I felt an instant attraction. . . .

I am in the vegetable patch, wearing a low-cut peasant's blouse with floral print skirt, cradling a French wooden trug in one arm. The trug overflows with multicolored beans, just picked from one of my towering bean teepees. My husband gazes upon me and approaches, as a slight breeze tousles my hair and my skirt flutters against my legs. My *amoroso* says he cannot wait until dinner to sample my cooking. I offer him a bean and he lustily bites the tip. The names of the beans roll off my tongue seductively — *'Purple Trionfo Violetto,' 'Yellow Romano Burro D'Ingegnole.'* We look at each other and then the bean teepee. I feel his hand, so rough yet so gentle on mine . . .

*Yuck!* Alice had nudged her cold wet nose into my palm. "Stop it," I scolded.

Oh, well. In reality, I'd be wearing blue jeans, a dirt-stained shirt, and sandals smudged with chicken manure. I'd be irritated that I barely had enough beans for a side dish, and furthermore, I'd botch the pronunciations so terribly that even I wouldn't know what I was trying to say.

I turned the page to cucumbers. Cucumbers were so erotically charged I could barely buy one without blushing at its reputation. I wasn't alone. Andy once told me of a time in the produce aisle when he "just happened" to notice a very attractive woman as she moved toward the cucumber bin. As she approached the cukes, most of the male eyes in the vicinity zeroed in on her (including his, I observed). Now here, I thought, was also an area where names could count. But before I could improve on the ones the catalog offered, I noticed the spread with melons, the female counterpoint to cucumbers.

Under the selection of watermelons, I found an Amish heirloom that exuded romance. 'Moon and Stars' was large, deep green, and sprinkled with yellow spots, like constellations. Some of the spots were larger, moon-like. Each melon was a wet, sweet piece of heaven that you could hold in your hands.

The catalog cantaloupes ranged from the tiny-bosomed, one or two-pound 'Jenny Lind,' to the voluptuous five-pound 'Magnifisweets.' A cornucopia of melons, one for every preference. I drift off again. . . .

I'm on a picnic with my man, on a blanket near the bank of a secluded pond. We shed our shoes and our cares as we watch the fish jump, the dragonflies mate. Everything is easy, lazy. A jug of wine, a loaf of bread, a sweet, juicy melon, and . . . we kiss, a long slow summertime kiss. Our thoughts turn to indulgence in more of life's pleasures, right then and there. I lean back and . . .

"MOM!" a hair-raising yell yanked me back to the kitchen. It was my darling daughter, informing me that her just-as-darling sister had hit her.

Here, then, was the maternal side of melons, pregnant — *so* pregnant — with *responsibility*. I knew well what passionate abandon could lead to — the fruits of love, cherub-faced fruits, yelling "Mom" from the next room.

Oh well, it was time to finish the seed order anyway. I smiled in spite of it all. Gardening is sometimes described as "an old lady thing." An old lady thing? Digging the fertile earth, enjoying the warmth of the sun, watching the birds and bees . . . Gardening is about loving, nurturing, touching, smelling, tasting. It is sensual.

Even more, it's sexual. Flowering, reproducing, fruiting — these are the primal acts of *life*.

Oh yes, I nodded, as I sat at my kitchen table on a frosty Colorado morn with my favorite seed catalog. Gardening is *the* sexiest hobby.

# Swarm Story

Tony kept calling me Marsha.

"Look over here, Marsha," he beckoned. My attention was fixed on the activity going on above my head, so I didn't look over until he called again. Then it dawned on me — he thought *I* was Marsha. I understood the mistake. Although he'd helped me dress just a few minutes ago, he didn't know me. We'd just met the night before.

I turned on the ladder, where I balanced seven feet up underneath a white pine and looked down. The wind blew slightly, cool and crisp, typical for an April morning on Colorado's front range.

A few feet above my head hummed a swarm of five thousand bees.

I smiled down at Tony, even though it wouldn't show from behind the veil, and Tony took my picture.

\* \* \*

No, I wasn't cheating on Andy; I was taking part in another adventure that spring, learning about honeybees. I'd always liked insects, and bees were a favorite — they were attractive, industrious, and socially complex. They lived in amazing hive-cities, and they created one of nature's most perfect, delicious foods. While I wasn't a beekeeper yet, my curiosity and obsession with gardening had been leading me in that direction. The previous spring, for fun and education, I'd attended a Beginning Beekeeping class, held by the Pikes Peak Beekeepers Association. The two days of instruction covered everything from bee anatomy to honey extraction, but what really made my antennae stand up was the session on swarm capture. From what I learned, capturing a swarm of bees was a profitable, nearly risk-free venture — and as easy as stealing candy from a baby.

145

\* \* \*

A jolly, bearded, ursine man by the name of Mike presented the session.

"The primary reason swarming occurs is overcrowding," he said. "To keep the hive healthy and to increase their population elsewhere, they divide."

He went on to explain that they begin the process by producing a new queen for the existing hive. Nurse bees feed a few of the larvae royal jelly, and the larvae grow, soon entering their final metamorphic stage into adulthood. The first queen bee who hatches from this metamorphic stage usually wins, by dispatching her still-pupating rivals; in fact, a queen's stinger is used only for that purpose. But even before this, the old queen, who first had food withheld from her so she'd stop laying eggs and then was further harassed by her hive-mates so she'd get down to a trim flying weight, has left with at least half of the hive.

Since it can take several days to find a location for a hive and settle in, the departing bees gorge themselves on honey. They're so stuffed their bodies are taut, making it nigh-impossible for them to curve around and sting. The binge also renders them docile. Often, the swarm will land within one or two hundred feet of the old hive, and they'll hang on a tree or shrub branch together, with the queen protected near the middle, while scout bees make a final decision on their new hive location. During a warm period, they release and fly together to the new digs. While the entire process can stretch out over a period of several weeks, the swarming itself usually occurs during a single day.

"All you really need for a capture, if the swarm is in a convenient place, is a couple of cardboard boxes with lids," Mike said. He stroked his dark beard nonchalantly while looking around the class, a diverse group of young, old, and middle-aged participants. He savored our surprised expressions. "I use boxes, the kind reams of paper come in. You can also use an empty hive super, which is the box-like section of a commercial hive. Of course, any openings have to be duct taped. Then, if the swarm's in a bush near the ground, where it's easily accessible, you can just put the box directly underneath it, give the branch they're hanging on a good jerk, and they fall in." He grinned. "It's like one bee's holding onto the branch and then someone's holding on to her, and so on, in a big chain, so when you shake it and the one lets go, they all let go."

Our group chuckled.

"Within a few minutes the remaining bees will form a smaller cluster, so have a second box on hand to get those. You can even have a third box, but normally the bees that are left will return to the hive."

He told how he typically wears only a veil for protection (no gloves or suit) while capturing a swarm. "The bees are sluggish from all that honey," he said. "They're really almost incapable of stinging you."

He talked about bait hives that bee catalogs sold to capture swarms. "They don't really work very well, but I found something that does. It's a huge paper pot with a lid that you hang from a tree with wire. In it you place a lure, artificial queen pheromone, which is also available through the catalogs.

"The scout bees will find the pot and look around for its queen, but won't find her. They'll measure the pot, to make sure it's big enough, then they'll report back to the swarm that they've found a home. Two years ago, I captured five swarms this way, but when I tried to use the queen pheromone again a year later, it didn't work. Apparently, it has to be fresh."

Mike said the Beekeepers Association worked with the County Extension Office, the Department of Wildlife, and the Humane Society each spring, taking calls from frantic homeowners who had discovered a swarm on their property and wanted something done about it — immediately. It didn't matter that the bees would leave on their own in a day or so at the most; the swarms were perceived as a serious threat. So, he or another beekeeper on the "swarm list" would go out and capture the bees to add to their own colonies. Mike said it was fun to have people watch, impressed with his apparent bravery.

"One morning I got a call," he told us. "There was a swarm at an elementary school, in a bush near the front door. By the time I got there, they had several classes standing out on the sidewalk to observe. I decided to give them a good show. There I was, standing close to the swarm, showing them my beekeeper's suit, veil, and gloves, taking my sweet time putting them on, all the while talking about the bees. After I finally dressed, I turned to begin the capture, and the bees," Mike snapped his thick fingers, "took off just like that." He laughed a deep belly-laugh. "I had taken too long. Boy, I can tell you, that *was* impressive."

By the end of the presentation, all I could think was, *This is so cool. I want to capture a swarm of bees.*

* * *

I had to wait another year before I had a chance. I attended a meeting of the Pikes Peak Beekeepers Association, knowing it was almost swarm season and the beekeepers would be putting together a swarm list. I wanted to be on that list. The meeting, one of only four each year and the first one I attended, took place at a neighborhood church. After the used beekeeping equipment sale in the parking lot, the 30 to 40 members and their guests moved inside. As we settled into our folding chairs, waiting for the meeting to begin, I listened to the two men talking in the row in front of me.

The older of the two, who looked to be in his seventies, was thin and grizzled. He wore loose faded jeans and a worn madras print shirt. "The tree was taken down," he said, in a tone loud enough for surrounding beekeepers to hear, "and about five hundred pounds of honey was recovered."

"Five hundred?" said the man next to him. He was nice looking, neatly dressed, and appeared to be in his mid-to-late fifties, just a little younger than my dad. He paused for a moment, considering. "You'd have to scrape it off, then filter it. There'd be a lot of junk in it; dead bees, stuff from the tree."

"One time I captured a swarm in the woods, then found the tree it came from," said the old-timer. "I knocked the tree down and took the rest of the bees with the honey. Later I cleaned up the honey and fed it back to them."

The buzzing quieted down as the president of the Association opened the meeting. He asked for guests to introduce themselves, and when it was my turn I told the group that I was a writer and gardener. I said I had attended the beekeeping class the year before and was interested in observing a swarm capture.

I took my seat, and the two men who had been talking turned to me.

The 50-something younger of the two whispered, "There's a swarm by the Country Club. We're going to capture it tomorrow. Do you want to go?"

"Sure," I answered, stunned by the immediate gratification of my heart's desire. The man introduced himself as Tony and drew a map showing how to get to his house. He said he'd call me by 8:00 A.M. and let me know if the bees were still there. He said he had a veil I could borrow and instructed me to wear light-colored clothing.

\* \* \*

The next morning, I awoke early, excited and thinking about the swarm, hoping it was still there. I dressed in khakis, cowboy boots, and a long-sleeved white shirt. In the class, we'd been told beekeepers wear white clothing because bees don't like dark colors; big dark shapes outside of the hive look too much like hungry bears. Moving on with my toilette, I discovered that for deodorant I had only a natural brand, honeysuckle rose scented, or lavender talcum — both no-no's in beekeeping. They'd mentioned this particular commandment in bee school as well. Do not perfume thyself before bee handling; be mindful of all scents, even those in hand lotions.

I knew from personal experience how much they were attracted to floral scents and didn't wish to take the chance of arousing even honey-sedated bees. My bee/perfume schooling had taken place in fifth grade. It was springtime, and I was sitting at my desk while a bee explored the surface of my hand. A few kids shrieked, "Look, she's letting the bee crawl on her!" I patiently waited for her to leave, and she did, flying out the window. My teacher, Mrs. Bernie, asked if I was wearing perfume and I admitted I was, something floral and secretly borrowed from my stepmom's dresser that morning.

That wasn't the first time I'd been up close and personal with bees, either. At age six, in one of my many Ellie Mae Clampett-style adventures, I discovered the fun of trapping them in baby food jars. I even got my sister Karen, who was a year younger, to join me. It was an exciting game, tracking the little creatures as they landed on dandelions and then slowly lowering the inverted jar over them, sliding the metal lid underneath. I'd stare at them in their little glass prison, mesmerized by the buzzing sound that came so loudly through the holes I'd punched in the top. The bees were always perturbed; it was as if they were giving me a good cussing. Nevertheless, I enjoyed the sensation of my power over the bees, even while experiencing a definite prickle in my conscience that what I was doing wasn't really kind. We always let them go — after a little while. That particular game ended when my little sister fell and cut her hand on a glass jar and Mom put a stop to it.

As I prepared for the 8:00 A.M. call, I thought about how, in the beekeeping class, we were taught to move calmly and slowly around the bees. Bees didn't have great eyesight but responded to the threat of motion near their hive. I could handle a zen-like state, the floral-free requirement, and the light clothing. People who panic easily would not be doing this anyway, I mused, envisioning the cartoon image of a person running away from a hive, a swarm of bees following in hot pursuit.

Tony called. The bees were still there, and I could come right over. Driving down a picturesque road to a subdivision sandwiched between the country club's lush green grounds and towering white sandstone bluffs, I found Tony's two-story brick colonial, with he and the other beekeeper out front, standing by a late-model truck. It was 8:40 A.M.

150

"Sorry I'm a little late," I said as I closed the car door, my camera over one shoulder and a notebook and pen in hand. "I had a hard time getting out of the house this morning — had to tend to the kids, you know."

"Oh, that's all right," said Tony. He nodded at the camera and notebook. "You'll be too busy for those, though. We thought we'd let you hold the bucket under the swarm. It's just next door, in the backyard of the house next to mine."

"Sure . . . okay." I smiled while my mind raced at the magnitude of the comment — as in, this changes everything!

Tony led me to his tidy garage where he had the gear: a veil, rubber gloves, and a white jumpsuit made of paper, all ready for me to put on.

"I got this from the place that makes chips," he said, handing me the jumpsuit.

Still dazed by my change from observer to swarm-capturing participant, I wasn't quite with it mentally. My first thought was, *Huh? Potato chips?* A second later I thought, *No, you idiot, computer chips.*

I took the suit and stepped into it, pulling it easily over my clothes. Yes, I thought, this could be a little Microsoft outfit. I'd never thought of the similarity in dress between beekeepers and chip makers. Then Tony handed me thick orange gloves to put on while he tied strings around my pants bottoms, making them bee-entry proof.

Tony handed me the pith hat/veil combo and then helped me with the long strings of that too, carefully bringing one under each arm, crossing them in the back, then coming around to the front, tying them around my waist. The experience had a sweetness to it, as if I were a little girl being carefully dressed by her father.

Then he took a picture of me standing by his garage and I just felt silly.

"I feel a little overdressed," I said from behind the veil as I trudged through his front yard. I was a space-girl, a chipmaker, a bona fide bee-person. What about all the stuff I'd learned about the impossibility of being stung?

"No, you're fine," Tony said.

We walked to the backyard next door. Tony's partner and the homeowners, a pleasant-looking middle-aged man and his wife, stood about 25 feet away from the pine tree where the swarm had congregated, on a branch about ten feet off the ground. There were two ladders set up underneath the tree, two five-gallon "bee drums" (modified paint buckets with lids), and a shop vacuum. Tony's grizzled beekeeper friend looked to be wearing the same faded outfit of the evening before, along with rubber gloves and veil. I was puzzled by the shop vac until the old-timer explained that he used them in swarm capturing, his own invention.

The homeowners greeted us. They were ready for the show. At some point Tony called me Marsha, and I, in another dimension entirely in my bee suit, thought he was talking to someone else. The atmosphere behind the veil was dark and isolating, other-worldly, adding to the surrealism of the event. I learned that the swarm came from one of Tony's two hives.

I went to the tree, and there it was, the first swarm I'd ever seen, 10 feet above my head. It was beautiful. There were actually two clumps on the same branch, one about the size and shape of a football, the other shaped the same but about one-quarter the size. Pulsating and java-colored, the bees hung amid fresh green pine needles, lively but relatively quiet. I'd imagined something larger, something much more menacing.

After taking a couple of pictures, I asked the neighbor lady, "Does it bother you at all that there are beehives next door?"

"Oh no," she said. "I give them sugar water."

Her husband smiled in agreement.

The older beekeeper, who Tony called Rev, walked to the tree; he was ready to begin. I handed my camera to Tony and followed.

\* \* \*

Tony took my picture, then Rev handed me a bucket and lid. "I'll get the big clump with my bucket. You hold yours right under mine, and put the lid on it when the bees fall in."

We climbed the ladders and positioned ourselves. Rev gave the limb a shake.

"There they go," said someone from down below.

Many bees fell into the bucket, but hundreds didn't.

"Now they're starting to move," I heard someone say. The voice seemed far away.

Bees started flying, buzzing, covering my veil, my gloves, my clothes.

I tried to absorb all the sensations around me, while quickly and carefully getting the lid over the top of my bucket. When I did it, the lid was upside down. My mind raced, *Oh, no! I screwed it up!* I couldn't turn the lid over for fear the bees would escape. On top of that, I was experiencing a major adrenaline rush.

I climbed down the ladder with the bucket and told Rev about the lid. Rev nonchalantly turned it over and sealed it. I looked at him through a veil blotched with bees. He was covered in them too; there were bees flying all around us, on top of the buckets, on the ladders, on the ground. *How many did we get?* I wondered. It seemed like a zillion still buzzed around.

Rev turned on the shop vac and began vacuuming bees off me, then I did the same for him. I told him about the bee inside his veil, near the back of his head; he said he knew. There wasn't anything either one of us could do about it anyway, not yet. It felt weird to suck up bees with a vacuum. I tried to be as gentle-yet-swift as possible. My emotions were definitely mixed — I was aware that some were probably being injured, but I was also determined to do my part as a member of the *homo sapiens* bee team.

"I'm going to vacuum the rest of the bees out of the tree," said Rev.

I looked up to see they'd returned to form several very small clumps. Rev climbed up the ladder, and I held the machine while he worked. When he came down again, we repeated the process of vacuuming each other, then the containers and ladders. I saw many bee corpses on the ground, the ladder, and my clothes. Some were squished, but many seemed to have died for no apparent reason. Their bodies looked abnormally large, full and taut, just like Mike had described in bee school. "I feel so sorry for the bees," I said. "How many do you think were killed?"

"We've probably got about five thousand — what's a few here and there?" Rev replied.

He was obviously excited, like me. In spite of the carnage, I shamelessly thought: *This was fun! I want to do this again!* I was back to age six. At that moment it was all about the rush of facing nature and claiming superiority over it. It was purely animal, even more, purely human. We were the tamperers, in the middle of everything, and wild with the excitement of it.

A few bees flew around while I helped Rev pack up. He had already shed his gloves and hat. Then I went back to the garage to take off my costume. My long hair was partially in my face, had been since I'd descended the tree the first time, and I hadn't been able to push it away. The thrill had died down by then. I had had enough of the bee suit.

By the time I had undressed, Rev was gone and Tony had returned to the garage. He confirmed my suspicion that the capture was messy. "If we had waited awhile, they would've formed one larger, longer swarm. You can usually just work your bucket right under them, practically place the whole swarm in it. And I give the branch one good hit, I don't shake it. The best way to do it is to cut the branch off and bring it straight to the hive. That way you'd probably have no deaths, but of course I couldn't do that here."

"What about the vacuuming, does it hurt them?" I asked.

"Naw, not really."

"And what's the likelihood we got the queen amid all that?"

"Oh, about 99.9 percent."

"Really?"

"Oh, yeah."

I asked about Rev, who had taken the bees and left.

"I just met him last night," Tony said. "I joined the Beekeepers Association about four years ago, and last night was the first meeting I'd been able to attend. They've always fallen on dates when I've had other engagements. By the way, Rev's a reverend."

"You're kidding!" I said. "Another surprise. I thought you two were long-time buddies."

"Nope. Never met him until last night."

I wondered at the loose communities we humans could create. Join up with some strangers who share a common interest, go out and wrangle some bees. So unlike the structured bee communities. The bees worked with the flow of nature; we seemed intent on making nature work with our flow.

Tony told me he got into beekeeping when his daughter was in junior high and they decided it would be a good science project. She soon went on to other things, namely, horses, and he kept with the bees. He showed me the barrel-like, three-foot-tall, stainless steel honey extractor in one corner of the garage that he'd bought used for five hundred dollars. "Even with this state-of-the-art piece of equipment, it's a time-consuming project every fall, extracting and bottling the bees' work," he said. When I asked him if he sold his honey, he said most of it went to his friends and neighbors, as gifts.

We took a quick tour of his orderly backyard, where I admired his vegetable garden with PVC bean trellises, a pond with a spouting carp fountain (Tony said the bees liked to drink from it), and in the furthest corner, two white hives, wood boxes on stands about two feet off the ground. The hives looked non-threatening, just a working part of his garden and a positive addition to the surrounding ecosystem. As we walked up, Tony pointed out the half-dozen or so bees crawling on the landing boards near the hive entrances and said, "You see, Marsha, it's still cool, so there's very little activity right now. Later on, it'll warm up and they'll start flying."

We'd been busy bees that morning, but, in fact, humans aren't anything like bees. I wondered what type of flying insect we might best compare to. Sure, we had cities like bees and drove our cars and flew our planes along predetermined paths that resembled the flight patterns of bees, but that's about where the similarities ended. If there were a species of unusually self-centered insects, ones that believed in community but were pretty much loose and free, and did whatever the heck they wanted — well, then, we'd have our mascot.

I thanked Tony for the experience, got his phone number in case I had any more questions, and we parted.

I never told him my name wasn't Marsha.

# Stove Love

It was spring cleaning time, stove-scrubbing time. Our stove hailed from the 1930s. A metal plate located inside her, just below the burners, declared her a product of The Eureka Steel Range Company, O'Fallon, Illinois. She was obviously top-of-the-line then, as the plate informed me she complied with "National Safety Requirements," but her ability was sorely lacking by 21st century standards.

She did the basics. Barely. The top four burners were set too close together for cooking with more than one large pot at a time, and a few of the holes in the burners were always clogged. The oven did a fair job, even though the door didn't close right (requiring a cardboard shim), and it wasn't insulated very well. The temperature regulation was, well, just a little flaky.

Her porcelain enamel finish was far from perfect. A dozen or so round chips, from dime to quarter size, marred her surface. But she was beautiful to me. In fact, I'd loved her since the first time I laid eyes on her.

She stood on four, nine-inch tall, curvy, cast iron/porcelain enamel-plated, buttercream yellow legs. That color also graced her doors, sides, and the four-inch tall curved back panel. Her secondary colors were two tones of sage green, a darker background with lighter streaks, in a faux marble pattern. The trim around the edges and Bakelite burner knobs were black, and fancy white porcelain pulls that opened the oven, broiler, and drawers dangled like earrings from chrome plates.

Not only was she colorful and curvy, but I loved her design. She was divided into two parts. On the top, one side had four burners with a faux-marbled cover and storage drawers below. On the other side, above the oven and broiler, was a flat work surface. There, you could place a hot pan or set a Mason jar full of wooden spoons, whisks, and spatulas.

The most wonderful aspect, though, was not her Art Deco looks. She held memories. I first time I saw her was when I was still a teenager, visiting my future brother- and sister-in-law's house for Christmas. It was 1980, and Danny and Victoria were children of the '60s. They lived in a Victorian-era cottage with groovy thrift-shop finds: fringed throws on their worn velvet sofa, faded Oriental carpets, shelves full of mismatched floral dishes, and assorted curiosities such as a brass perpetual calendar hanging on the kitchen wall and a racy early-1900s nutcracker in the shape of bare, booted female legs sitting in the coffee table's nut bowl. I loved the artsy recycled romance of their home and Danny and Victoria's easy-going hospitality.

As I watched Victoria pull a roast goose from the oven, I admired the stove. Victoria told me it came from Goodwill. They'd paid 20 dollars for her.

A few years later, Andy and I were buying our first home, and Danny and Victoria were moving from their cottage to a 1920s bungalow. They now had a young son, Victoria had a college degree, and they were moving closer to the mainstream. I learned that the person who bought their house was going to turn the half-acre lot into a scrap yard. I felt sickened that the beautiful cottage-style garden Victoria spent years creating would be destroyed, and I panicked when I heard they had left the stove.

"You have to get that stove," I said to Andy. Fortunately, he felt the same. He contacted the new owner, who was happy to trade the treasure for our boring white Magic Chef. I felt like I had rescued a piece of family history.

* * *

I got to work, scrubbing the oven with the soapy steel wool as I listened to Elvis, our rescued tufted canary, twitter and trill at the chickadees he saw from the living room window. As I cleaned the front of the stove, I noticed the skinny light green streaks that marred the marbled finish between the oven on the right and the storage drawers on the left. Andy had the best of intensions; he wanted to do

158

a thorough cleaning job on the stove after he brought her home. He'd just finished remodeling the kitchen and wanted to surprise me. He had no idea the cleaner would bleach the porcelain finish as it dripped down its surface. That was over a decade ago, and I still remembered the look of remorse when he told me about it.

I lifted the stove cover to get to the burners and glimpsed the warning stenciled in small red print: "Caution. Turn off gas cocks before placing this cover over burners." That brought to mind my half-sister Renea and how she pointed it out to me while bursting into laughter. That was well over a decade ago, too. Renea was experiencing some serious teenage rebellion and my dad asked if she could come stay with me and Andy for a while. We welcomed her that spring, and although there was an 11-year age difference, we became friends. A few months later, we were both older and wiser. She went back to Missouri, and I was left with fond memories of her ribald humor.

I scrubbed around the porcelain pulls (one pull, its chrome attachment piece missing, was in a drawer, had been for years), and thought of the Christmas dinners I'd prepared. Many of my firsts were cooked in this oven — first duck, first goose, first leg of lamb. The stove helped me prepare holiday sweets: hundreds of sugar cookies baked with my young girls, dozens of loaves of sweet breads and pans of baklava had emerged warm and fragrant from her.

As I cleaned out the compartment that held cast iron cookware, I studied the embossed maker marks on pots and pans. The cornbread mold, with a row of ears of corn, read *No. 273 Griswold Crispy Corn Stick Pan, Erie PA USA*. *Warner Ware* skillets hailed from *Sidney* (I assumed Sidney, Nebraska) and a very small, and, I think, very old skillet read *Martin Stove and Range Co Florence ALA*. They held not only the memories of cooking but of flea-marketing, searching for bargains to stock the kitchen, this stove, my life. I wondered who used those utensils, seasoned the skillets, before me.

I thought of the life I'd lived during two decades of cupcakes and gumbos. Andy and I shared the cooking with Zora and Lily, who loved the magic of turning wet batter into golden cakes, tossing and pouring ingredients into pans, stirring pots while they bubbled and steamed. One of their specialties was pizza. Lily, in first grade, would help me mix the dough while her sister made the sauce. Her recipe never varied: one can of tomato sauce mixed with fresh minced garlic and basil from our garden, and freshly milled pepper. We grated and chopped and sprinkled together.

I found it hard to believe that Victoria and Danny's son, Alex, would graduate from high school that year, and that Samantha was almost a teenager. We were always saddened to think how Danny didn't live to see them finish middle school. My half-sister Renea grew up, settled down, and found her perfect mate. She continued to entertain all who knew her with her bawdy humor.

I finished my task. The stove was cleaned and waited to serve, to bake the next loaf of bread, fry the next egg, or boil the next kettle of water for the next pot of tea — a slightly-battered but loyal helpmate on this ever-revolving world, a world where everything changes yet somehow stays the same. She'd become grimy again, and certainly become more weathered, at the same time helping to nourish us through tragedies and celebrations, a piece of the heart in the art of living.

# Green with Envy

The deal was done in two shakes of a lamb's ear. As the outgoing vice president spoke to the garden club, I whispered to Sri, "Do you want to trade?"

Sri's eyes got as big as dinner plate dahlias. "You *know* I do." She giggled like she'd won a small jackpot as we switched the gifts we'd just received for our service as garden club officers: I got her miniature pot o' rose with red flowers, and she took mine, with its coral-hued blooms.

I knew Sri wanted my rose. We were friends, and I was quite familiar with her current plant passions: flowering vines, variegated anything, and coral- or salmon-hued plant genitalia.

Our attention drifted back to the garden club proceedings. "Our reigning president has held a position many covet," vice-president Liz said. She stalled. "No, that's not right, because gardeners are not a covetous group."

I looked across the table at Sri. Her eyebrows rose in reply to mine.

Liz brought out our reigning president's departing gift, an Austrian copper rose in a five-gallon terracotta pot. This time, my eyes went green.

"Now this rose . . ." she began. I stopped listening, caught up in my thoughts. I'd read about this rose in Lauren Springer Ogden's book, *The Undaunted Garden*. It was one of Ogden's favorite roses; she called it both vibrant and xeric. I had marked it a "should have," but I was wrong; it was definitely a "must have." The fairly glowing blossoms, single-petaled beauties of an exciting coppery-orange color, transfixed me. I'd never seen quite that shade before in a flower, anywhere. And, oh, how the color of the pot set it off!

I wanted, wanted, wanted the Austrian copper rose, and I cursed the outgoing president's luck. I thought about volunteering for the post next year.

I admit it, I am covetous. I've yet to meet a gardener who isn't, and while I'm not proud of it, "I want" seems to be an integral part of our makeup. I want pretty flowers. I want fresh herbs. I want homegrown tomatoes. I covet my neighbor's arbor/greenhouse/goldfish pond/dwarf conifers/Hori-Hori knife.

That evening the vice of rapaciousness was in full flower. In addition to the officer's ceremony, we were holding a plant exchange. Upon arrival, we set our contributions outside the front door, eyeing the others' — plants that would soon be claimed in a polite, or as polite as possible, first-come/first-serve free-for-all. My tray of unmarked clary sage seedlings and bronze fennel babies in muddy two-and-a-half-inch pots joined an assortment of other pass-alongs: monarda, daylilies, Jupiter's beard, nepeta, a few tiny evergreen trees, houseplant cuttings. They were all the usual suspects, except for two. Heading the parade of flora like queens, a pair of gallon-sized pots held Spanish lavender in bloom. Their lilac butterfly-topped heads nodded royally. Murmurs wafted over them. "Wow." "Look at those." "Beautiful."

I wondered who would be the quick and greedy victor.

Probably someone with a passion for lavenders, or the color purple, or butterfly-shaped blooms, covetousness and passion being, after all, kissing cousins. For years I'd felt it ebb and flow, burn brightly and then burn out. My most recent fixation was for Harry Lauder's 'Walking Stick,' a filbert that Allen Lacey rhapsodized about in *Homeground*. I knew that this shrub, with its contorted, corkscrew-shaped branches, would look so amazing, so satisfyingly twisted yet handsome, in the winter landscape. *My* winter landscape. I remembered hugging myself the day Fortune smiled upon me and I found the Johnny Depp of shrubs at a discount chain. I pushed around my cart, showing off my prize, like a mom with her new babe. Not one, not two, but three women remarked on it, confirming my giddy feeling of conquest.

My enthusiasm dampened only a little that afternoon when Becky remarked that she'd seen "more of them dead than alive" locally. I proceeded to coddle my darling for a full year. He died anyway. That cured me, temporarily at least, of my obsession with Harry.

The curly filbert was only one in a long succession of intense plant lusts. Usually, I yearned for something tabloid-like: eggplants that looked like small white chicken eggs, freakishly small pumpkins, or carnivorous plants. My latest craze, for air plants, or epiphytes, lasted almost a year. Now I was into aloes and chartreuse flowers.

I found it funny, and not, how plant infatuation was much like the human-to-human variety. How exciting and romantic it could be to long for something or someone you did not possess. And then, after obtaining the object of desire, how surprising to discover mundane reality rendered the fun mostly gone. I still had feelings for former horticultural favorites, but it wasn't the same.

A friend of mine lusted, for years, after the 'Carol Mackie' daphne. To Edie, this shrub was everything a shrub could ever hope to be — compact, hardy, semi-evergreen, graced with tiny-leafed variegated foliage and endowed with heavenly smelling blossoms in the spring. After searching, fruitlessly, for a local specimen for sale, she did the unthinkable — she stole a cutting from a nursery plant that wasn't for sale. Guilt, combined with propagation failure, ensued. She obtained a second cutting, this one legally. Another failure. It didn't help that I had a small 'Carol Mackie' that I originally purchased in a two-and-a-half-inch pot for under two dollars. And for some reason, 'Carol' seemed to pop up in conversation all the time.

Me: "I visited the Horticultural Art Society's garden last week, and everything's coming into bloom!"

Edie: "I bet the 'Carol Mackie' smelled wonderful!"

On another occasion:

Edie: "Have you read Rob Proctor's new book?"

Me: "Yes. I loved the part about variegated plants; you know, he mentioned the 'Carol Mackie' daphne several times."

Finally, just this year, I tracked down and bought two more starts in two-and-a-half-inch pots. I gave them to Edie in hopes of shutting us both up. Days later, on Mother's Day, her family presented her with a big one. She officially has a lifetime supply. Quite soon, I suspect, she won't like them as much as she used to.

By the time the garden club evening ended and I'd helped with clean up, I'd forgotten about the plant exchange, and the lavender. As I headed out the door I saw the leftovers — some of my plants, a big pot of monarda, and a pot of daylilies. These were unmarked too, and I figured them to be nondescript.

"What are those?" asked Becky, who was taking another turn as president of the club that year. She pointed to the claries.

"Clary sage."

"Really? I need some of those." She scooped them up. "Why don't you take the other pots — we need to get them all out of here."

A few days later I spoke with Kate, the woman who had brought the lilies. She'd special ordered them for her gorgeous Victorian garden and found she didn't have room. They were a special variety with coral blooms.

I couldn't wait for Sri to see them.

# Rainbow's Bride

"She's going to kill him. You need to separate them," Mom said.

"I don't know," I protested. "Maybe I should check around, ask first."

I was on the phone with Mom, and she couldn't see what I saw — that the possibility of mortal danger had passed, at least for now.

"What I've heard," she said, in her slightly Southern accent, "is that they'll kill each other."

"But I don't want to take care of two bowls."

Ignoring my excuses, she said, "When I had that tank in Missouri, that's what the man at the pet store told us. And he was right. We didn't even have another *Betta* for him to fight with, but that didn't stop him, he started biting off the fins of the other fish!"

I imagined Mom loading the dishwasher (or doing something else, she was always multi-tasking), her blue eyes animated, her expression certain. We looked alike, but that's where it ended. She was hotness and surety; I, coolness and doubt. "This is different, Mom. I have a male and female. It's just the two of them."

"If she's chewing off his fins," Mom declared. "She's going to *kill* him."

\* \* \*

"Him" was Rainbow, our second *Betta splendens*, or Siamese fighting fish. Selected and named by seven-year-old Lily, he was last summer's spontaneous fish buy at a local big box. I approved the purchase for two reasons; one, she'd asked for a fish, instead of a toy, and I was a big fan of real-life experiences (hence all the pets), and two, our previous fighting fish did not live up to his name, at least when it came to survival. I figured Rainbow, handsome as he was

165

with his metallic blue and red coloration, would not be a long-term house guest.

To my surprise, he proved hardy. Lily's chore was to feed him, and I cleaned his gallon-sized, bubble-shaped glass bowl. Every few days Rainbow and I went through the same routine; I'd chase him briefly until I captured him in his original plastic cup. He'd react claustrophobically, fins waving, darting around like he was looking for the secret passageway out. While he waited in semi-panic, I'd swoosh out his habitat's fetid water, scrub the bowl, refill it (gauging the water's temperature by feel), add the magic dechlorination stuff, and slide him back in.

He always seemed pleasantly surprised at the change in pollution level, delighted with the new air bubbles. *It must be boring*, I'd think, *in that bowl every day*, though I'd read that *Bettas* actually thrived in tight spaces. A book I'd shared with the girls said that they were gathered from the street gutters of Thailand for export. Still, his life seemed lonely, uneventful, lacking.

I tried to make it more interesting. At summer's end, I floated a water hyacinth from our pond in the bowl. Rainbow swam among the tangle of roots until the plant decayed and I had to throw it out. Then I added a bare-root elephant ear plant, but it, too, fouled the water. Sometimes, between house and home-office tasks, I'd take a minute to tease him with the tip of my finger on the glass, making him follow it in defense of his territory. Approaching the pink, faceless invader, he'd spread his fins wide and flare his gill covers. Through the magnified glass his head became huge, in a theatrical fish-Kabuki way, and quite menacing. I thought about getting him a mirror so he'd have someone to challenge daily, but changed my mind. Being on the alert is not the same as companionship.

We'd had him for almost a year when Andy brought home a trio of bamboo cuttings he happened to find in the markdown area of the grocery store. I added them to the bowl, thanking Andy for the Far East plants, a clever addition.

"That bamboo should only be in an inch or so of water," my mom pointed out on her next visit.

By summer vacation, our daughters had another strategy: we'd search for a real companion for Rainbow, a girl *Betta*, a mate. On the big day, Zora, eleven, had her turn; she would choose Rainbow's bride. She selected a small peachy-white fish with short blood-red fins and gill slits. Though not as peacock dramatic as the long-finned males of her species, she had two unusual markings – a small black spot on her back, near her tail, and an opalescent blue patch just under her dorsal fin. The girls named this charming female Cloud. I secretly hoped she'd be as hardy as her bowl mate.

I tidied the bowl for their big date, and we gently delivered her into the clear water. Immediately, Rainbow flared his gills and fins and went after her, all fiery red-and-cobalt fury. Cloud fled to the drab pebble-covered bottom and stayed there, very still, as if she were hoping to camouflage herself or fly the white flag, while Rainbow hovered above her, brooding, majestic, his draping fins floating beneath him, conjuring a Japanese silk kimono. Each day we checked to see if she was moving around freely. Rainbow would not let her. The male *Betta*, a merciless bully, chased her anytime she dared to stir, his gills flared, fins flashing, seemingly furious.

"Oh, he's horrible!" squealed the girls. "Get her away from him; he's so much bigger than she is."

"Let's wait," I said. Though I didn't voice it, I thought he probably wasn't that much bigger, though his fins made him appear thrice her size.

Once Cloud stayed so long at the bottom I thought her dead, but she was only, once again, playing fish-opossum. She seemed to have no injuries, but my conscience bothered me. Had I sent her to an evil fate? I imagined an Asian romance. Cloud, a young geisha, thrown into the fortress of a handsome, yet aging and cranky, samurai and forced to wed. *How she must despise him*, I thought.

Several days later, about a week after Cloud came to the bowl, the weather changed. Zora was the first to notice Rainbow's long fins. They looked shredded. Soon I witnessed Cloud in action. She chased him, nipping his long, lovely fins mercilessly with her tiny, down-turned mouth. When she made contact, he'd jolt, as if shot through with electricity. A part of me cheered for her, Rainbow's-bride turned bride-of-Frankenstein, but for the most part the display horrified me. I sprinkled in more dried bloodworms, their preferred food, wondering if hunger could be the provocation. No, her hunger was not for food. She chased him relentlessly, rarely giving him a rest. Over a few days' time, his fins became more and more ragged, like silk kites tattered by a treacherous wind. I wondered if he bled, if he felt pain.

"You should separate them," the girls cried. Now they were on the other side, witnessing the havoc one small damsel could wreak.

"Maybe I will," I said.

\* \* \*

While my mother often gave sound advice, she wasn't always right. After our "she's going to kill him" conversation, I decided to seek an expert opinion.

The girls and I visited a nearby pet store, and I cornered a clerk near the aquaria.

"Um, I'm not really sure how they get along, the males and the females," said the pasty-complexioned teenager. He wielded a fish net, scooping out goldfish for another customer, who had a turtle to feed. Zora and Lily were a little upset about that. "The only thing I can tell you is that I know a lady who collects *Bettas*, has a whole row of them on her fireplace mantle in their little bowls. She says she moves them around if they don't get along, and lots of times they don't."

*Okaaaay*, I thought, *that tells me a lot*. The fish-catcher smiled politely, hoping I'd be satisfied. I pressed him for more information, but he had no more to offer. The book I had at home gave no insight either. While it may sound macabre, I had a secret scheme. I wanted to see how the water opera would play out. Would Cloud go as far as trying to kill Rainbow? Would I be able to rescue him in time if she did? Sick or not, I wanted to find out, so I held my breath and kept watch.

Over the next days, Rainbow's fins grew shorter and shorter, until they matched Cloud's in size. Just as I expected, he wasn't much larger. Then one afternoon he seemed sluggish. A guilty queasiness washed through me. *This is it,* I thought. *He's mortally wounded, and I'm responsible. I have caused this.* All that afternoon I was miserable. I knew, without a doubt, that the ASPCA or PETA would be justified in hauling me off to animal-cruelty jail.

Then, the next morning, the barometer changed again. Rainbow seemed fine. My gloom lifted as I watched them swim to the top together, side by side, for their feeding. Practically chummy.

"I think the fish are getting along," I told Andy as I peered into the fishbowl after breakfast, "now that his fins are short."

"Now that she's castrated him, you mean," replied my mate, who up to this point had been mute on the whole unfolding drama. I watched him sitting at the head of the table, drinking coffee, reading the paper. He took a sip from his mug and grinned at me.

"Ha, ha," I said. "Yes, it probably doesn't have anything to do with equality." Our 20-year marriage had taught me volumes about the male-female power struggle. At times I would feel almost sympathetic toward Andy, in his own fishbowl with a trio of regularly dramatic females (and mother-in-law). Then, I'd come to my senses.

As I watched the *Bettas*, optimism filled me. Sure, the honeymoon was a little rocky, but it seemed like they may have settled into married life. I noticed something else. Cloud seemed to bulge a bit around the middle. *It's probably my imagination,* I thought, and didn't mention it.

Several hours later, on the phone with Mom again, discussing the pros and cons of letting elementary-aged children watch PG-13 rated films, I happened to glance at the bowl. Rainbow was draped over Cloud, his body curved as if in rigor mortis.

"Oh, no," I said, jumping up from my chair in a panic. "Something's going on with the fish."

"Is he dead?" Mom's voice echoed my alarm, with only the slightest tinge of I-told-you-so anticipation.

I hung up and raced to the bowl. Rainbow's body was indeed curved, arching over Cloud's, and, upon closer observation, I saw that she was turned upside down, her body curved as well. Together they created the image of a yin-yang, each embracing the essence of the other. They seemed motionless, except for the tiny quivering of Rainbow's tail fin. Soon they separated and Cloud, now lying sideways, motionless and curved as if in a state of paralysis, began to drop whitish tiny eggs from her vent.

As they drifted down, Rainbow, now completely animated, swam below her and caught them in his mouth. One, two, three, four . . . he gathered them, then headed upwards, where he gently blew them out on the top of the water. There they nestled in a line of translucent bubbles that had not been there that morning. Again, the fish came together in their yin-yang embrace, again the eggs were dropped, gathered, and gently placed in their bubble nest.

During the mating, I called the girls in to see.

"Mom, this is *gross*," Zora said.

"Oh, it's sorta interesting," said Lily.

"It's *beautiful*." I sighed, caught in the wonder of it all.

The egg laying went on for a couple of hours, until scores of tiny roe encircled the bowl.

All along we had been witnessing not an underwater prelude to murder, but an intense courtship. I knew now that I had sensed something strangely familiar in the love dance, one of seeming aggression, one that brings a male and female together for their ultimate purpose — the creation of new life.

I stood at the bowl and smiled, pleased that I had followed my instincts, and honored to be a witness in this marriage among the fishes.

# The Miracle of the Angel(fish)

The temperature outside read six degrees as I sipped my morning coffee and brooded about Christmas and shorter, colder days. The year had not been a banner one. Besides the horrendous, soul-strangling wars in the Middle East and the never-ending political strife in our country, my family had personally suffered the deaths of two members, my Grandma Love and my Aunt Beverly. We'd also lost our beloved cat, Merlin, to old age. Now it was Christmas. I'd been scanning strangers' faces, and they mirrored mine. Stressed. Scroogy. A friend, Rain, who managed a toy store, said she dreaded the season. "Every year, when we run out of sale items, at least one person says, 'You've just ruined my kid's Christmas.' "

I thought about pettiness and ugliness — the stupid, ongoing argument over whether to say, "Merry Christmas" or "Happy Holidays," the story about a peace-sign wreath condemned by a homeowner's association in the local news. Then I noticed our 50-gallon aquarium near the window. Three palm-sized angelfish stared at me, as if trying to communicate. I checked the floating thermometer, and my heart jumped. It was at 50 degrees, the cut-off point between dangerously cool and dead tropical fish. Somehow, the heater had become unplugged.

I plugged it in and added hot water, hoping the angels would be okay. Then I settled once more into dark thoughts about this holiest season of high expectations. Carols and hot chocolate weren't going to cut it — not this year.

As the fish warmed up and became active, I remembered how for a couple of months this summer I'd thought about giving them away, along with two canaries, three rabbits, and five chickens. Once fodder for life and writing, the whole menagerie now seemed, after seven years and several tragedies, as worn out as I felt. Still, I'd been

171

unable to give them up, animal friends who, in their own quiet ways, had brought so many joys and insights.

We had started our 50-gallon aquarium with two small angelfish and a few other species (neons, mollies, platies, cherry tetras and a Corydoras catfish). When the angels reached maturity, we discovered we had a male and a female. Regularly, they spawned. Our family watched, delighted, as they performed an aggressively beautiful mating dance, laid hundreds of eggs, and guarded them fiercely from the other fish. When the eggs hatched, the parents hovered over their tiny fry. About a week later, the babies disappeared. This cycle was repeated several times before my curiosity got the better of me. I spoke with a breeder and learned that they had not been eaten by their parents. They had *starved*. If I wanted to breed them successfully, I'd need a second tank where the fry could be fed a special diet of brine shrimp.

I decided against the second tank, though the thought of the couple's hopeless endeavor haunted me. Then one day we noticed a survivor. A minuscule swimmer, unmistakable in his diamond shape, riding the tank's gentle current, bobbing around the leafy vegetation. Thrilled, we rooted for him. As he grew, I wondered how he'd found the nourishment to flourish in spite of the odds. I named him Miracle.

One frozen Colorado morn, I decided that our family of three fish would serve this holiday season as my personal Herald Angels. Their message was clear. If they could weather loss and harrowing events, if they could survive and flourish despite what seemed like great odds, then, surely, so could we.

# Our Gender Bender Hen

One morning at chicken feeding time I decided to check our girls' legs for mites. It wasn't something I did often, but there had been a case the year before, and I wanted to be on top of things. I eyed them as they pecked at their breakfast, a mix of grain and dinner leftovers. The black-skinned, partially feathered legs of the two golden Silkies, Flora and Fauna, looked smooth and healthy, as did the legs of Athena, our sweet Rhode Island Red. Even Mrs. Bush's gams (the rather homely Bearded Araucana that we picked up two years before) looked all right. Then I got to our black- and white-speckled mixed-breed hen Aphrodite. The seven-year-old hen's legs looked fine too — except for the spurs. Yes, spurs, those long, claw-like things roosters fight with. Aphrodite now had one on the back of each leg. My eyes traveled up to her head. She had also grown long, dangling wattles and a huge red rooster's comb.

I stared in disbelief. She'd been crowing for a few months, but I had heard that hens would sometimes do that. This felt unreal. It was as if I had just seen Broonzy squeeze out a puppy. Impossible. I had held this chicken's first egg in my hand over six years ago; it was streaked with blood from the effort, something I found poignant, wondrous even. We'd eaten her eggs for years. Lily even witnessed her lay one. As a resident of Colorado Springs, an evangelical Christian stronghold, my first thought was Salem, Massachusetts, circa 1600. As a lover of all things green, all things animal, I was an admitted nature worshipper; heck, I could probably be labeled a non-practicing Pagan. Could I be accused of witchcraft? Or, even worse, could this be some kind of an environmentally-caused mutation?

It felt very *Twilight Zone*-ish, breaking the news to my family. Andy went into immediate denial, suggesting that I was somehow mistaken about the chicken's sex (for seven years!?!); Zora, now 13, responded with a rather sarcastic, "Oooohh-kaaaaay." Lily laughed out loud; Aphrodite had always been awful. Haughty, domineering, and gorgeous, ever since her arrival she'd been our most beautiful and least liked chicken.

After several days, in which a supernatural aura continued to hang over our home, I sought help. I sent short emails to several universities that specialize in the Poultry Sciences. In reply, Dr. Wallace Berry at Auburn University wrote: "Sex changes, such as your hen's, are fairly common, especially in older hens. This happens when something damages the ovary, usually a viral infection. The remaining ovarian tissue tries to grow back but takes on some of the characteristics of both ovary and testes. In fact, it is referred to as an 'ovotestis.' It will secrete testosterone, which makes the hen appear and behave as a male. However, she (he) will not be able to effectively produce sperm or sire chicks."

Well, there it was. A logical biological explanation. The chicken wasn't enchanted, nor did she make a conscious decision to go butch; it just happened. The incident made me think about that first egg with its crimson streaks, religious debates about sexual orientation, and how mysterious our world is. What babes we are in understanding it, in understanding ourselves. Aberrations in nature *are* the norm. And the scientific proof was indisputable — Aphrodite transformed into Hermaphrodite, without any hocus pocus at all.

# TRIOPS!

The small box, displayed near the checkout line, screamed kiddie fun: "TRIOPS From the Age of DINOSAURS" "Watch their AMAZING AQUA-BATICS." The graphics showed two T-Rexes hulking near red cliffs, a pterodactyl soaring above, and the triops, in the foreground, swimming in a water cloud. The triops resembled horseshoe crabs with antennae and forked, whiplash tails. Through artistic perspective, they looked T-Rex size. A *Land of the Lost* adventure — for only $3.99.

"Can I get it, Mom?" asked Lily.

I frowned, recalling '70s-era sea monkeys, nothing more than shrimp eggs sold as an amazing family of naked half-human, half-alien cartoon creatures with fins, tails, and what looked like crowns on their heads. The packaging had shown the family playing tennis and promised that you, too, could enjoy their amazing performances in *your very own home!* Mom sea monkey wore lipstick and a blonde flip hairdo like Marlo Thomas in *That Girl.*

At least these triops seemed closer to reality. *What the heck*, I thought. *It's about nature, about learning. A fun summer experiment.* I never said no to anything in those categories.

Back home, Lily hatched some of the eggs in a plastic cup. (Cup, spring water, and lamp not included.) She fed the brood with "hatching nutrients," and we waited eight days for them to grow big enough to move to their kidney-shaped pool. During this time, we educated ourselves: Triops are crustaceans that have survived for 240 million years, making it through times of drought by suspended animation (or "diapause"). Like sea monkeys, they're a type of shrimp, but these are commonly called tadpole shrimp. Triops means "three eyes" — which we would surely see, eventually, hopefully, once they grew. The box said they can grow up to three inches in length, sometimes doubling in size in a single day. They

175

have between 35 and 71 pairs of legs, through which they can obtain oxygen while swimming around (feet-breathers?). Oh, and they can be cannibalistic! Gross! Secretly, though, I wasn't too disappointed to learn that 90 days is a ripe old age for triops.

By the end of eight days, only three scrappy survivors were left from the nine hatchlings. (Cannibalism happens.) One was about a quarter-of-an-inch long; the other two were a little over half that long. It was almost time for Lily to move them to their new habitat.

* * *

Doing dishes in the kitchen, I heard a blood-curdling scream. "I KILLED THEM!"

I ran to Lily's room to find her in tears, metal spoon in hand.

"Try to calm down. Tell me exactly what happened."

Her voice shook. "I put the spoon in to catch them. I caught them on the side of the cup. And then, I CRUSHED THEM!"

240 million years of evolution wiped out by a tablespoon.

"Oh, sweetie, I'm so sorry!" I looked into the cup. "You still have the big one. . . ."

The last of the triops liked his new home. He swam, he twirled, he somersaulted through the plastic pool, entertaining us with his many-legged aquabatics — exactly as promised. Although eerie, he was also, somehow, cute. Sadly, a few days later, he died too. We had no clue why.

"Lily," I said, "we have more eggs and food. We can try again, set up a small aquarium, use a real heater."

But her heart wasn't really into it. Neither was mine.

Lily insisted on a burial. As we stood in the garden, paying our last respects, I experienced another flashback from my childhood. In the 1970s, one of the big food companies marketed a brand of margarine through a series of TV commercials, featuring Mother Nature, a seemingly gentle middle-aged woman with daisy-crowned hair and a long, flowing white dress. The commercials opened with Mother Nature doing something extraordinary, like strolling through a jungle with an elephant, or reading to a group of forest animals gathered around her rocking chair (all real animals, no CGI back then). Then an off-camera person would present her with a slice of bread spread with margarine. Mother Nature would take a bite, and her face would radiate pleasure. She'd rave about her delicious, sweet and creamy creation, butter, until the narrator interrupted and informed her that what she tasted was, surprise, margarine. At the news, Mother Nature's smile turned into a mask of fury. She raised her arms to the heavens and proclaimed, "It's not nice to fool MOTHER NATURE!" Thunder boomed, lightning flashed, the earth quaked, and all the terrified animals ran for cover.

This experiment, hatching and housing prehistoric nature in a plastic tub with some bottled water and a lamp, was definitely on the spectrum of trying to fool Mother Nature. And it worked out about as well as can be expected.

# Summer Lovers

The affairs began within a week of each other. After 20-some years of marriage, Andy and I were surprised to find ourselves ensnared by others — he with his wrong-side-of-the-tracks trollop, me with my beautiful Mexican lover.

I could not help falling in love with Tulio. His eyes, my God, wonderful espresso eyes that gazed — no, bored — into mine with such romance, such intensity, such devotion. He had it all, a personality that drew women wherever he went, yet an ability, when we were alone, to make me feel as if I were the only one. I knew I wasn't, that he belonged to someone else, but I didn't care. Our time together was ecstatic. Caresses, kisses, nuzzling . . . his mouth on the buttons of my blouse, first pulling playfully, then urgently. Once, his tongue darted into my ear and . . . *electrifying*.

My husband's lover was different. Oh yes, she was beautiful. She possessed a taut, lithe young body, and she poured her attention on him like molasses on a buckwheat pancake. Yet, she was *common*. I knew her type, and it was legion — gorgeous young, ordinary old. She'd call, bitchy and demanding, and he'd jump. He thought her demands were "cute." He showered her with gifts, while I looked on, jealous, but mired in my own guilt. My husband wasn't Elowen's only love either, but, like me, he knew and didn't care. He reveled in the attention, worshipped her youth.

We knew about one another's infidelity, and we flaunted our summer loves.

One afternoon my husband caught me and Tulio nuzzling on the bed. I looked up and smirked, as if to say, "He's *so* much nicer than you, you cannot imagine."

"He's cute," said my spouse, "but not what I'd call a *real* dog. A Chihuahua . . . Good grief."

"Only three-quarters. Don't forget the miniature pincher." I planted a kiss on Tulio's tiny head and he turned his melty eyes toward me. "Mmmmm, puppies are a girl's best friend. Your feline, on the other hand, she's a mutt."

"Elowen? Aww, she's a sweetie." At the sound of his voice saying her name, slinky grey tiger Elowen leapt upon the bed and brushed up against my husband, gently scent-marking him with her velvet cheek.

*Tart*, I thought.

Zora and Lily came into the bedroom, catching us in the act. "Hey," said 10-year-old Lily, "why don't you get your own dog if you like ours so much?"

"Here, kitty, kitty," her 13-year-old sister, Zora, beckoned.

Elowen ignored her owner; she had spotted Tulio. She raced to him. Delighted to see his playmate, Tulio bolted from my arms, tail wild with excitement. The two began their routine, one we'd seen dozens of times. They began to roll and tumble, taking turns pinning one another down, biting with gentle vigor. Two four-month-olds, more interested in one another than any of us.

As we watched them absorbed in their play fight, I thought about the one that my husband and I had indulged in this summer. Our little mock rivalry had been fun, serving to awaken the youngsters still very much alive in both of us.

Ah, there's nothing quite like middle-aged puppy love.

# Bug Heaven

I was thrilled to learn that my seven-year-old nephew, Sean, was into bugs. You see, Zora and Lily did not inherit my "creepy crawly things 'r' fun" gene. While we'd shared a few adventures with insects, the girls still generally winced at earwigs and were squeamish around spiders. I, on the other hand, had adored spiders since *Charlotte's Web* and always felt comfy around the six-legged, eight-legged, hundred-legged . . . you get the picture.

One Saturday morning, Sean brought over his latest acquisition, a no-legged pet slug. "I found it under a rock yesterday."

"Oh, cool," I said, peering into the container. I felt relief to see the mollusk was small (slime *is* a little gross) and alarmed to see it resided in a tin, on a bed of grass. "Let's get it some lettuce and mist it," I said. "They like to be cool and wet."

The slug still looked overly sluggish after our efforts, and I made an unfortunate remark: "Sean, I'm afraid he might be visiting slug heaven really soon."

Sean didn't take my comment well. In fact, he was upset. Really upset.

To make amends, I proposed an Ellie Mae-style adventure: "Want to go to a bug museum?"

That made him feel a lot better.

Within the hour, we turned off Highway 115 at a 10-foot-tall Hercules beetle. We headed down a dirt road to the May Museum of Natural History, a place I'd been longing to visit for years. Now, finally, I'd found someone to join me!

I wasn't sure what to expect. I'd studied museum work in college, even interned twice at the Colorado Springs Pioneers Museum. I knew museums could vary wildly, from a roadside trailer to the Guggenheim. What we found on this day was a charming 1940s adobe building. We entered and bought tickets. Past the gift shop was a large exhibit room filled with display cases that held approximately eight thousand invertebrates, about a tenth of their collection; a collection which was considered to be one of the world's most outstanding. Nothing high tech, no slick design, no interactive games for the kids, just glass cases, much like you'd imagine in a Victorian library or a curiosity shop, filled with treasures collected mostly from the tropics. The odd combination of science and antiquities quickened my pulse. *Oh, how I love this*, I thought.

I didn't even attempt to stay with Sean. He fluttered randomly about the room, much like one of the tropical insects. "Wow, this tarantula eats birds!" "There's a HUGE fruit bat!" Though excited, I moved in an orderly line, more like an ant (pun intended), trying to absorb the contents of each case. We saw: Columbian beetles so large that, in flight, they can break street lights and knock down men; giant locusts with rainbow-hued wings; huge Brazilian butterflies in metallic greens and blues; a stick insect, 17 inches long; and leaf insects from Borneo and Madagascar that were replicas of the leaves they rested on. I found myself not in a museum so much as an unusual temple devoted to evolution and beauty! The art before my eyes mocked anything man could ever hope to create: transparent butterflies lovelier than stained glass, gold and silver beetles that could make a Tiffany silversmith weep.

I wanted to hug each and every case.

In the gift shop, I asked about the fall closing date, October 1st, and said, "I've really got to come back one more time before then."

"Can I come, too?" asked Sean.

I smiled at him. *Boys could be so fun!* "Of course!"

Back at the house, we found that the slug had succumbed, another reminder of how man's efforts at species domination can fail so easily. We gave the slug a burial in the flower garden, saddened, but also solaced by our very own glimpse of Bug Heaven.

# Housekeeping from Hell
## (or That's not a Spiderweb; That's a Science Experiment)

My sister-in-law Amy said a very strange thing to me on Christmas Day. She and her husband were guests the night before, for our annual Christmas Eve dinner, one of the few times during the year in which I clean the entire house top to bottom, cook a gourmet dinner for a crowd, and decorate. She said they had admired how everything was so well put together: the meal (lamb-you-can-eat-with-a-spoon, roasted vegetables, garlic potatoes, salad with citrus), the buffet of sweets, (including a Yule log cake, figs stuffed with almonds and ginger, and fancy chocolates), the candlelight, Andy's great-grandmother's transferware china, the damask tablecloth, the silverplate and crystal (most from Goodwill), the real Douglas fir decorated with vintage ornaments and cranberry and popcorn strings. I even had scented soaps that looked like big peppermint candies in the bathroom.

"You're very domestic," she stated, with what I took to be a tinge of envy in her voice.

Obviously, she didn't know me at all. I loved creating beauty, I loved cooking (most of the time), and I loved to share these things with friends and family. But, honestly, all this spit-shine and glitter was an aberration.

Here's reality:

Our house is always cluttered, stuff strewn on top of almost every available surface. The buffet is covered with mail, kids' toys and homework, maybe a piece of clothing or two, and a litter of miscellany. Same goes for the top of our lovely built-in bookshelves, the coffee table, and any other flat surface. The bathroom usually smells a bit like pee (we have an "if it's yellow let it mellow" policy), has an overflowing trash can, even though it's emptied almost daily, and the normal sink-grime is on a par with what one might find in a Texaco station (why a Texaco station, I'm not sure, but that's what I always think of, maybe because I grew up in the South). The bathtub usually has a ring. There are always spiderwebs — in the corners of ceilings and draping a light fixture or two. Ditto dust bunnies, though I prefer to call them ghost turds, like Stephen King does. There's animal hair here and there and most everywhere. Once in a while (rarely!), there may be animal pee or poo. One time our cat, Merlin, peed in the house, and Lily, playing near the place it happened, said matter-of-factly, "It smells like a zoo in here, Mommy." Yes, I was horrified. For a little while.

Our kitchen floor, a nice white linoleum with a small green diamond pattern, is often dirty with drips of coffee and other beverages, crumbs, and you-name-it. It gets mopped at least once a week and swept almost daily, but it reverts to gross again within 24 hours. The stove rarely sparkles. The refrigerator gets cleaned regularly, but that only lasts a few days as well, and the counter is usually littered with crumbs and splotched with jelly (compliments of Andy). Many times I have thanked my lucky stars that I live in Colorado, where *cucarachas* (cockroaches) are rare.

We don't have dirty clothes strewn about or dirty dishes piled up in the kitchen, and we're not hoarders, and we're not filthy, but on a day-to-day I often do the minimum in the tidying department. I was taught better, much better, than this. Everything in its place, make sure your underwear's clean in case of an accident, and what if the Queen of England dropped by? Even as a kid I'd think, *God, don't they know we're in America?* Both of my parents were tidy, but my dad's especially neat. He always taught us "never do anything half-assed, don't just hit the high spots, use elbow grease." That advice, in the housekeeping realm at least, didn't take.

I'm naturally on the grubby side, but I'm not lazy. I love to work, but I mostly love work as a means to a solid end — cultivating a garden, writing a book, building a fence, preparing a homemade meal, painting a room. Housekeeping, which can never, ever, ever, be completed, equals drudgery in my mind. Moreover, I see it as a political ploy to keep all the good sisters *down*. The truth is, I care much more about putting a vase of fresh flowers on the table than I do about dusting the mantle (or keeping a toilet bowl immaculate).

And you know what's odd? I love myself anyway, and I love my life. My kids have spent their childhood with pets and dirt, learning about biology and life and natural beauty. They're happy, hearty, and sick less often than any kids I know. I'm a believer that the antibacterial lifestyle, a scheme to sell more consumer goods, is actually making us sicker — and science backs it up. Look it up.

I'm messy, but not disgusting, or at least I never thought so — until a certain discovery. . . .

* * *

It was in November, and I was in my before-Christmas cleaning mode again. On this day, I decided to tackle a certain possum-belly table in the kitchen. This table, a yard-sale find about 25 years prior, was a sweetie. It dated from about 1910 and was smallish with a top about two feet high by three feet long, made of oak planks, covered in chipped white paint (which I referred to as *patina*). Underneath were two large, rounded, slightly dented tin bins, the "possum belly" part. Back in the olden days, when people used to bake all their own bread (if you can imagine such a thing!), these bins held flour and sugar. Now, in the early 21$^{st}$ century, I used one of the drawers for storing pasta — various kinds that caught my fancy, plain or herbed or spiced — in bags and boxes. I also kept packages of beans there. The bins often served like a black hole; impulse buys got sucked into them and then forgotten. A few days earlier, I had noticed a hole in one of the pasta boxes when I'd looked in the drawer. I knew it to be the work of the Indian meal moth, *Plodia interpunctella*, and decided it was about time to clean the possum belly table thoroughly. You may note that I didn't jump in right then.

Today was the day, though, deep cleaning day, and as I began pulling out boxes and cellophane-wrapped packages, a nightmare unfolded. Most of the cardboard containers, at least a half dozen, had

185

at least one worm or larvae hole, about the size of a BB, in the bottom. My face twisted in disgust as I found, underneath the boxes and packages, brittle, airy casings, the shells left over when larvae outgrow their bodies. Actual worm shit was mixed in with all this, in the form of dust. (I knew it was shit because I'd studied arthropods in the master gardening class. The proper term, if I recalled, was *frass*). SO INCREDIBLY GROSS! I grabbed a roll of paper towels and a bottle of environmentally friendly orange cleaner and set to work, groaning, "Oh my God" at regular intervals.

Apparently, the bugs couldn't get into the cellophane-bagged pasta, so I ran the sink full of hot soapy water and washed those. I started to save the infested pasta for the compost pile but was too disgusted. It all went into the trash can. Then I tackled the drawers themselves. After cleaning and drying the packages I ran another sink full of water and put the now-emptied drawers into them. I washed them thoroughly, set them on a towel on the floor to dry, then went back to do the underside of the table.

What I discovered there made me catch my breath — in amazement. I had discovered the rest of a small ecosystem! I had seen the ugly part, but this was something else entirely. Underneath the cabinet, attached to the drawer slides, I found a total of seventeen spider egg cases. Each of these was made of silk and suspended from silken threads, and each contained a spherical web ball. Enclosed in each silk ball were light dirty-yellow eggs — a dozen or so (I held them up to the light). When you do the math, that's a couple hundred spider eggs. Three very fat mama spiders were still alive, sitting near their nests, and some of the nests had dead remains, of daddy spider I'm guessing, clinging to them.

*Wow*, I thought, my self-loathing forgotten for a moment, turning instead into wonder. *This is Spider City! Hell, it's spider-frickin-metropolis!*

I was fascinated. Spider City came about from the ample food they found, in the form of the Indian meal moth larvae, which in turn were fed by the pasta products I provided. It was so cool. I took pictures and looked up the spiders. They were *Cheiracanthium mildei*, a.k.a. sac spider, a.k.a. prowling spider, a.k.a. yellow house spider, often wrongly identified as the brown recluse, which has a poisonous bite and a fiddle shape on its upper exoskeleton, or carapace. Mine were not yellow, but tan, and I read that sometimes they are green.

I came back from my book and admired Spider City for a few minutes before I commenced with its destruction.

It wasn't easy to play Old Testament God. I felt remorse about removing the spiders and their progeny. I didn't actually kill anything in an obvious way, but scooped up the webs, spiders, and eggs with paper toweling, and placed them gently into the trash can, which I then took to the dumpster. Maybe they'd survive the trip to the dump and hatch in the spring, but probably not. At least I could fool myself into thinking they had a chance.

I'm animal-tolerant (at this point, that goes without saying), but I do require a certain balance. My personal limit is when the critters get the upper hand. This also applies to gardening and the weed ratio. Sometimes it feels like a battle between good and evil, which is a quandary for me because I'm never quite sure which side is which.

It's easy to slack off on bug control in Colorado, the Land of Few Bugs. It's not like warmer, wetter climates where cockroaches, ants, mice, and other pests thrive. In fact, we'd only had an issue with cockroaches that one time, in our first home. We set off bug bombs then, something we'd never done before and haven't done since. I learned in the Master Gardening class on pesticides that insecticides are nerve poison and not good for anyone.

Through the years, I'd also learned that some cleaners could be killers — of the bad *and also* the good.

Clean is very nice, but a little neglect can be just dandy. While many consider a discovery like mine shameful, I choose to interpret it as an innocent, unexpected, and tuition-free lesson from Mother Nature, a glimpse into the inner workings of an ecosystem.

# Zen Doggie

Lily, 11, and I were out on a walk when we were startled by a yell, "Hey, your dog's in the road!"

We turned to see a man in black spandex slowing down on his bicycle. He nodded at a mutt headed our way.

"He's not ours," I yelled back.

The rider shrugged and pedaled off. The dog lumbered up. A big mutt with a sweet face, floppy wheat-hued ears, and fur clipped close on his torso for the August heat. From his looks, I guessed maybe St. Bernard and German Shepherd. "Hi, there, boy," I said. I gently grabbed his collar, noticed the dry patches of skin on his back. *Eewww.*

"What's his name, Mom?"

"Don't know, Lil." The tags jingled in the quiet Sunday afternoon. "There's only a license and rabies tag."

I didn't want to end our walk when we were only two blocks into it, and I wasn't keen on corralling a non-threatening but perhaps mange-ridden dog with our own. Surely, his owner would be cruising the street soon, calling for him. I'd been there, so had most of our neighbors — a temporarily unlatched gate or open door was an invitation for your dog to split. I released him, and he padded purposefully in front of us. A slight limp and scrawny hindquarters said he was an old guy. I was pretty sure he wouldn't do anything stupid.

He stuck with us. A block down he wandered into a yard with two women, one holding a baby. The young mother smiled until I said, "He's not ours." Then she clutched her baby to her chest. I'd alarmed her. *Sorry,* I thought.

We walked, and the dog led, pausing every now and then to hike his leg. Then he lagged behind, then he led again. The blocks passed, and Lily and I didn't talk much — the dog commanded our attention. In a gravel parkway, he stopped and squatted, leaving loose stools. "Oh, gross!" we exclaimed together (now I *really* didn't want to take him home).

We continued. He paused to sniff a calico cat under a Jeep. A pretty blonde teenager smiled from the porch. "Oh, he's cute," she said.

"Not ours," I told her.

Everyone noticed him, no one felt compelled to take him under their care.

Soon it was time to head back home. He'd been with us nine blocks; we had a mile to walk back. When we stopped at the corner, the dog kept going. "He'll probably keep going," I whispered.

"Bye," Lily called.

"Why did you do that?" I scolded. We turned around and crossed the street, putting distance between us and Tag-along. But he spotted us and ambled up again.

Lily grinned. "Looks like he *is* ours."

"If he follows us home, I'll find his owner," I told her.

We passed the girl on the porch again.

She laughed. "He's *still* following you?" In a last attempt to shake him, we crossed the street again. It didn't work. I knew he had to be thirsty. First thing I'd do when we got home is give him a bowl of water, if he followed us home.

Two blocks from our house, he crossed the street and disappeared.

"That's where he joined us," I said to Lily. "He's going home."

I was glad to be rid of him, but happy for his company. What was the nature of Zen Doggie? A mysterious geriatric escapee, or a serene, mystical visitor? The answer was clear. Just a fellow traveler, joining us for a Sunday walk.

# Supernatural Estate

The decision to go to the estate sale that morning was spontaneous, based on fifth-hand email information, *but there were supposed to be books*. Specifically, "a great deal of gardening, botany, and entomology books — $2 hardback, $1 softcover."

To a major nature- and gardening-book freak on a budget, those words made for one sweet carrot. After calling to make sure there were some left (I was told there were still "hundreds"), I hit the road.

Off Colorado Springs' Highway 83 I took a bumpy, still-icy-in-spots dirt lane that meandered through greening Ponderosa pines. "No Trespassing" signs bobbed by as I met people leaving the sale in their SUVs and extended cabs. They pulled over, made room for my Taurus. The anticipation and excitement built as I got closer to what might be a good score.

The excitement ebbed when I entered the handsome Spanish Colonial home. The reality of the sale hit home. The sad and simple truth struck me as vaguely obscene — those who attend estate sales were invited intruders, shuffling through the material details of a lost loved-one's life. They were there to see if anything struck their fancy, if others' loss could be their gain.

In the foyer, a woman sitting behind a table greeted me. We chatted; she told me the deceased had been a naturalist. I was directed to her personal library.

I noticed the rocks first — piles of mostly unmarked specimens scattered across a huge brick hearth. The sight put me at ease. I, too, collected rocks (and nothing says nature is a passion like rocks strewn about one's home). I had to look through them, too, but the reason I came was *books*.

Browsing the shelves, I was reminded how intimate and telling a personal library is. Paper and ink reveal passions, amusements, and concerns: the head *and* the heart. Mine stirred to realize this woman

191

was a kindred spirit. Such wonderful books! I saw a book on seashells, one on feathers, and so many more that celebrated Nature's extraordinary physical designs. To my growing pile, I added books exploring the minds and souls of animals. I thrilled to discover a vintage copy of *The Harvest of the Years* by Luther Burbank, and it was a godsend to claim a recent dictionary; mine was in tatters. I found a book on Einstein, Willa Cather's *My Antonia,* and Mark Twain's *The Jumping Frog.* This lady and I not only shared a love for nature, but our tastes merged in other subjects.

Most of the books were marked in. I would be able to see what she found most interesting and whether it meshed with my own perceptions. We could almost converse! Soon I had a stack of about 30 books, and I still had the minerals to explore.

"Are you a member of the family?" I asked the woman at checkout, hoping to express both my condolences and gratitude.

"Oh no," the woman said, looking embarrassed. "We're just handling the sale."

I perused the books when I got home, selected a few to read right away, and lovingly added the rest to my bookcases.

A few days later, as I headed out the door to pick up Zora and Lily from school, I grabbed one of the books, *Earth Prayers from Around the World.* A few minutes later, parked and waiting in the car, I thumbed through it, giving special attention to the dog-eared pages. My attention stopped on a poem circled with thin red marker. The first line began, "Do not stand at my grave and weep."

The poem, by Joyce Fossen, described how the spirits of the dead live on in wind, rain, sunlight, and starlight. The very last lines read:

*Do not stand at my grave*
*and weep.*
*I am not there. I do not sleep.*

Underneath, my benefactress added her own two lines of verse:

*Do not cry–*
*I did not Die!*

I caressed the casual red script of my newest acquaintance. Spirits *could* live on in wind and sun. They could also live on, and even communicate with those of like minds, in secondhand books.

## Supernatural Postscript:

Not long after this day, I told my story about the estate sale on a local radio show. By that time I had discovered, from address labels in a couple of the books, that they had belonged to a woman by the name of Gloria Barron. When I looked her up, I realized that I had met her son, the author T.A. Barron, at a writer's conference a few years earlier. He'd been there to speak and to promote his new book, *Tree Girl*. I had purchased a copy. Gloria's son was a writer of YA environmental fantasy — and I was there to seek a publisher for my first novel (also a YA environmental fantasy), *Zera and the Green Man*.

I didn't contact Barron when I made this discovery. I didn't want to intrude so close to his mother's passing.

Several years went by, and then Eric, an English professor friend, asked me if I might have an essay or two to share with his summer class of writing students. I went through my work, found "Supernatural Estate," and thought it might be a possibility. Eric liked it and thought it would also be an interesting post for his blog, *U.S. Represented*.

I decided it was time to look up T.A. Barron and tell him about the essay. I sent him a message on Facebook, along with a link to the essay.

This was his reply:

*Sandra, thank you so much for sending me your message as well as your essay! I was very moved by your description of my mother's books — especially the poem that caught your eye. There is no doubt whatsoever that you and she were — and are — kindred spirits.*

*Growing up in that home you visited for the estate sale was like growing up in an enchanted wonderland of nature, ideas, discovery, and love. You* understand, I can tell! On top of that, the wonderland was ruled by a natural teacher and eternally young spirit, my mother, Gloria Barron.

Let me also tell you this little story. The day you sent your message to me, I was visiting some schools on the Western Slope. Just before I was about to drive back to my home in Boulder, a Rocky Mountain Bluebird flew over and sat right opposite to me. That bird, more than any other creature, reminds me of my mother. She always admired the iridescent blue wings, of course. But she also admired that bird's independence — since Rocky Mountain Bluebirds fly singly, not part of a flock, she felt a kinship with her own individualism. (She'd look at those birds and say, with a twinkle in her eye, "There goes an individual like me.") As soon as I got home I checked my mail — and found your message. So, your timing was perfect! Gloria was right there, in the air, with us both. And I do believe that she was smiling to know your experience with her books.

By the way, how did you figure out that Gloria was my mother? Good sleuthing on your part! I'm delighted to know that you, like me, are a storyteller. And I certainly like the title of your book. All I can say is that I wish you success in sharing that story with others — for there is deep joy in that sharing.

Attached is a photo of my mother. I think you'll be able to see her love of nature and all our fellow creatures by the way she is looking at that golden eagle. The eagle is not alive (because it was being delivered to the "Touch Nature" museum that my mother created at the Colorado School for the Deaf and Blind, so that those kids who couldn't see could still feel the wonder of an eagle's wing and many other examples of wildlife). Yet even though the eagle is no longer alive, the connection that my mother felt for it is clear. Thank you again for your kindness in sending me your essay. I wish you all the best in life and in your writing!

Warm wishes, Tom (T.A. Barron)

# Diamond Dog

One early December morning, a newspaper ad caught my eye: "Teacup Chihuahua puppies, $300." Zora had been asking for her own dog, a companion breed, like Lily's Chihuahua/miniature pinscher, Tulio, and so I called the phone number. When I learned that the puppies were only a few blocks from our house, I became excited. Surely this was a sign!

Zora, 14, shared my excitement. As it was a Friday and a school day, I made the executive decision to let her skip school. In our house, the school attendance policy is as follows: "If your grades are A's and B's, you can skip all you please!" While some were critical of our ways, I didn't let it concern me too much; this parenting policy was backed by none other than David Bowie in one of our favorite songs, "Kooks":

*And if the homework brings you down*
*Then we'll throw it on the fire*
*And take the car downtown*

After taking our car to Manitou Springs and dropping Lily off at middle school, Zora and I headed back to our neighborhood. Soon we were standing on the porch of a forest-green two-story Victorian. The gentleman who answered the door wore regular clothes — jeans and a white, long-sleeved, button-up shirt — but his looks and demeanor were a combination of the Vampire Lestat and Slash of the rock group Guns & Roses. He was thin and pale, with longish, pointed, carefully manicured fingernails, and chest-length curly black hair. He introduced himself and his voice was soft, welcoming. "I'm Jasper. You must be here for the puppies," he said, brushing a long strand of hair from his face.

I introduced myself and Zora. "The puppies are in the kitchen," said Jasper. "Follow me." We followed the bare-footed man as he padded down a narrow hallway to a spotless and undecorated kitchen. In the middle of the linoleum floor was a little metal fence corralling five puppies. Tiny and blond with white markings, they were scrambling around, bumping into each other and interacting as puppies do. The pen contained an upturned cardboard box with a blanket inside for sleeping, and two bowls, one with water and one with puppy chow. There was no sign of the mother. Zora's face lit up, and Jasper extracted a cigarette from a package in his shirt pocket. He lit it, took a drag, and let it dangle from his fingers.

"It's okay, honey. Go ahead and pick one up," Jasper said to Zora as he blew out the smoke.

She selected the biggest, handsomest puppy. Our neighbor took another deep drag from his cigarette and exhaled. "Oh, I'm sorry. That one's spoken for." He frowned and added, somewhat wistfully, "Unfortunately, all the puppies are *males*. I prefer females."

I nodded, but raised my eyebrows, thinking, *Why?*

Zora picked up another puppy. "This one's cute!" He was smaller than the first, with white markings on his head, feet, chest, and the tip of his tail.

"Yes, he is," Jasper agreed. "And that one's very special. He has a *diamond* on the top of his head."

I nodded again, thinking, *Well, that spot's sort of diamond-shaped. . . .*

Zora cooed over the puppy, petting and talking to him as Jasper watched, smoking. By that time I was harshly judging Jasper's smoking around the puppies. I also wondered if anyone else lived there. The big house seemed so empty and quiet.

"Where's the puppies' mother?" I asked.

Jasper waved his free hand toward the window. "I put her outside."

As I looked over the other three puppies, and asked Zora what she thought about them, Jasper watched and smoked. I didn't feel like pushing the issue of seeing the mother — the pups looked healthy, and, besides, three hundred dollars was an amazing price for a teacup Chihuahua.

Zora scarcely looked at the other three. She'd made her choice, Diamond Dog. "Can we get him?" she asked.

Not to appear too eager, I asked Jasper if he'd consider taking two hundred and fifty dollars, and a check.

"Sure, I'll take two-fifty," he said, putting out the cigarette in an ashtray near the sink, "but I have to have cash."

"We'll make a quick run to the bank then. It shouldn't take more than fifteen or twenty minutes."

Jasper extracted a second cigarette out of the pack, smiled, and gestured toward Zora. "She's welcome to stay here, if she wants to."

The fingernails, better cared for and longer than my own, caught my attention again. Jasper seemed harmless, but my mommy instincts, twisted by Hollywood popular culture, flashed to Buffalo Bill in *Silence of the Lambs*. *Oh, HELL no.* I thought. *I would not be leaving my 14-year-old daughter alone in a strange man's house. Under any circumstances.*

"Thanks for the offer, but Zora can run into King Soopers and get some puppy food while I go next door to the bank. How does that sound, Zora?"

\* \* \*

We arrived back with the cash, and Diamond Dog jumped up on the fence when he heard Zora's voice. *Oh my*, I thought, *he's already bonded with her!* The puppy wagged his tail; he was ready to go.

Back at home, we sprung the news on Andy, who wasn't exactly overjoyed with our impulse buy. Yet, after a little grumbling, he warmly accepted the new addition, even cuddling with him for a few minutes at lunchtime.

After lunch, we took the puppy to a spay and neuter clinic for his vaccinations. The vet tech gave me a weird look when I introduced the puppy as a teacup Chihuahua. "I don't think so," she said. "Maybe part Chihuahua, but that face says terrier." Zora and I traded looks as she continued, "And he's too young for shots. You'll have to bring him back. He doesn't look more than five weeks old."

Only five weeks old, and a fake teacup! Oh, Jasper! *Well, I thought, that explains the cost, and why he wasn't keen on showing us the mother.* Zora and I weren't upset, or even that surprised; we were mostly amused that Jasper had succeeded in pulling a fast one.

You see, our Westside neighborhood was full of interesting characters. There was the sweet intellectually disabled man we saw regularly who always wore a Superman T-shirt. He would sometimes run down the street in a burst of enthusiasm after imagined bad guys. Then there was the Westsider I called the "Be Positive" man, known to others as "Wagon Man." He walked around pulling a train of children's wagons filled with stuffed animals. He also carried a large American flag and wore a "Be Positive" sandwich-board sign. He waved and smiled at everyone, and many of us waved and smiled back. In a house a few blocks east of us lived a senior citizen who was the spitting image of Kris Kringle. From early childhood, the girls knew the big Victorian as "the house where Santa lives." "Santa" worked at the North Pole, an amusement park up Ute Pass.

Notable neighborhood pets included a tame squirrel who rode around on his male owner's hat, the lady down the street who had a noisy parrot on her porch in the summer, and a husky that pulled his teenager around on his skateboard. Jasper would henceforth be known as "Puppy Scammer." We wouldn't confront Jasper or try to take the pup back. We'd bonded with him, and besides, we felt sorry for him. Sold too young and exposed to all that secondhand smoke! It was good we rescued him!

We took Diamond Dog to the middle school that afternoon when we picked up Lily. A small group of excited kids surrounded us, hopped up on the opportunity to hold a puppy (like what kid wouldn't be, right?). We handed the puppy to Lily first and he peed on her. The kids hooted. Looking back, I imagine that was probably a semi-terrifying experience for the puppy, all those kids and all that noise. Looking back, I think maybe that experience at least partly explains how his personality unfolded.

# DIAMOND DOG

\* \* \*

Over my loud and persistent protests, Zora decided to name the tiny mutt Chancho, after the cute little chubby boy in the Jack Black comedy *Nacho Libre*, a movie she and her boyfriend were obsessed with. She said she didn't know what "chancho" meant in Spanish. (Later I'd learn that was not true.) I knew because I had looked it up. "Zora," I said, "Chancho means 'pig' — as in 'filthy, disgusting, gross.' Please give him a name with some dignity!" My pleading had no sway. Zora had made up her mind.

Chancho grew into seven pounds of exactly what the vet tech predicted him to be, a terrier/Chihuahua mix. His build was stocky, and he had stiff short fur, except on his face, where he had long, semi-bushy eyebrows, a mustache and a beard, and a longer strip of fur going down the center of his head that you could finger comb to create a doggie Mohawk. This long hair ran from the top of his head and down the entire length of his back. The fringe of back hair could be pulled up for a "razorback hog" effect. Because of his facial fur (which you could not trim, as he would try to kill you) I sometimes affectionately called him "Beardy." His other nicknames included "Nacho," "Nano," "Baby Naner Thing," "Little Billy Goat Gruff," and "Tasmanian Devil," but mainly he went by Chancho. His looks, perennially puppy-like, inspired endearments. His terrier face featured a slightly off-center black button nose and round coffee-colored eyes, accented with those bushy eyebrows. Once, as we sat in the waiting room at the veterinarian's office, a middle-aged woman saw Chancho and exclaimed, "Oh, what a cute little dog! That face is just to DIE for!"

Looks are deceiving. Chancho looked sweet, and he could be sometimes. But, to put it indelicately, Chancho was kind of a dick. When the woman in the waiting room made the comment, she had no idea that we'd just come from a ferocious fight in the examining room. It had taken three technicians to hold Chancho down for a vaccination and nail clipping. He finally had to be fitted with the tiniest of muzzles, one about the size of a large man's thumb (I didn't know they made them so small). The muzzle infuriated Chancho, and he continued to growl and choke a bit on his mustache, part of which had gotten into his mouth. I flashed on *Silence of the Lambs* again — this time on Hannibal Lector in his bite mask.

Chancho's aggressive behavior extended to all strangers, as well as people and animals he knew well. He was the poster-child of annoying little dogs — a barker *and* an ankle biter. If a visitor was spared the ankle attack and trusting enough to try to pet him, he would snarl and lunge. This is not to say he couldn't warm up, eventually. For instance, one evening Yolanda, our animal-loving neighbor down the street, came over to watch *Downton Abbey*. Chancho greeted her at the door and, predictably, went for her ankles. Yolanda, nonplussed (and wearing jeans and sturdy shoes), laughed. "Oh, you silly boy!" She sat down, and Chancho began to approach her, repeatedly. She would try to pet him, and he would bark and nip. She would laugh and say a few more words to him. The nips quickly turned into gentle love bites. Yolanda continued to interact with him, and it wasn't long before Chancho jumped onto the couch and snuggled up to his new girlfriend.

Jealousy was Chancho's primary negative emotion. He behaved horribly at feeding time (even though he had always been well-fed and had his own bowl). If he felt you gave another pet too much attention, he would show his hurt by getting on your bed and urinating on your pillow. He attacked Broonzy, and Broonzy was more than 10 times Chancho's size. Broonzy was usually patient and kind; the one time he lost it was when Chancho nipped him on the testicles. For a moment, Diamond Dog saw his entire life flash before his eyes.

Chancho loved to hoard toys and other items in the folds of his bed, like a magpie. For a while he used to stash special items, like the occasional used Q-tip that just missed the trash can. Then, when he reached adolescence, he would knock over the trash can to obtain used feminine hygiene products. We had to get a Chancho-proof container.

I partly blamed Chancho's grossness on the name Zora had given him (names matter!), but I felt the irritable demeanor might just be a lack of empathy. He certainly did not seem to have the psychic soul-connection Tulio displayed. Tulio, Andy and the girls told me, somehow knew when I was a mile away from home in the car — and that is when he would start waiting for me by the door. Tulio would follow me around all day when the girls were at school; it didn't matter if I was outside in the garden, in the bathroom, or at the computer, Tulio was there (or waiting outside the door). Tulio was the lover, Chancho the fighter.

At least that's how we thought it was until we left for 10 days, on the first vacation we'd had in years. Chancho, Tulio, and Broonzy stayed home and were looked after by a dog sitter who visited daily. She sent us videos, and the dogs seemed to be doing well (only Tulio pined, refusing to eat much for the first three days). We missed them a lot, and when we returned home, the reunion was ecstatic. Only Chancho held back. We could tell he nursed a grudge. We brought in the carload of luggage and spent ten minutes giving the dogs hugs, pets, and kisses. Then, as we had no fresh food, we decided to make a quick run to the store.

As soon as we shut the front door behind us, Chancho began a piteous crying, unlike anything we'd heard before, or from any animal. It was as if his tiny heart would break. We opened the door and comforted him, and when we closed it, he began to wail again. The girls stayed home while Andy and I went to the store. Our hearts in our throats, we realized for the first time that Little Billy Goat Gruff loved us more than we ever dreamed possible.

# The Audacity of Dirt

I was in for a ride, and I knew it. Putting together a neighborhood fundraiser for Barack Obama (or, as we called it, a "Down to Earth Garden Tour") was going to take more than a few hours of volunteering. It was going to take planning, hard work, and a good chunk of my summer.

Yet, when my friend Beatrice came up with the idea, I didn't hesitate. "Sure, we'll be on the tour. I'll even help you put it together." We had plenty of time, two full months. My motivations, however, were mixed, both honorable and selfish. I wanted to help the campaign, and doing it through gardening seemed a custom-fit; but I also saw the tour as the perfect incentive to resurrect our backyard. Once a small urban paradise, our garden had been transformed into paradise trashed, by a decade of drought, Broonzy, and a defeatist attitude (what does a garden matter when our country's going down the tubes?). Now, inspired by Senator Obama, I felt the energy of a new era. Reviving our garden would be another metaphor for "Yes, we can."

The idea also seemed perfect because six months earlier Andy and I had salvaged about two thousand bricks and a dozen about-to-be-bulldozed rosebushes from a house undergoing renovation. A plan, a real garden plan, quite different from my usual fly-by-the-seat-of-my-pants method, had taken root over the winter in my imagination. We would turn our small 13-foot-by-20-foot lawn (actually a dusty area of dirt and weeds) into a bricked area. I'd weed and mulch the surrounding flower beds, prune the shrubs and trees, rework our tiny pond (now strangled by cattails), replant the rescued roses, add a few more flowers and some vegetables, and *voilà!* Our garden would be in order and more beautiful than ever.

A good plan, but not without its challenges. One major challenge was that Andy was a lifelong Republican. (Just think of us as an older and flabbier version of Dharma and Greg.) It took some persuasion to get him to see that one of the benefits would be putting to use those bricks we worked so hard to salvage. It wasn't for Obama, it was for *us*!

Needless to say, Andy was unconvinced. Getting him onboard took patience. It took cajoling. Finally, two weeks before the tour, when the paved area was only half-finished, it took, I'm embarrassed to admit, a hissy fit. Let me add this in my defense: on some projects, a hissy fit (as a last resort) is just how it rolls, for both of us.

To his great credit, Andy also helped me when I became a dame in distress with the pond. For years, our small, plastic-liner pond had been a sweet little self-sufficient ecosystem, containing escaped-from-their-pot-and-now-colonizing cattails, 25-cent pet store goldfish, and hardy red and white water lilies. That spring, when no goldfish flitted among the overgrown cattails or lily pads, I knew something had gone wrong. Terribly wrong. The fish had disappeared, and it wasn't because they were eaten by wildlife. Our dogs would not have allowed it. The pond was overgrown, something was amuck in the muck, and I had to deal with it.

Dealing with it came on Pond Cleaning Day. I tried to pull up a piece of the thick grass, thinking I could saw out chunks with my pruning saw. No luck. I heaved, I ho'ed, I wedged a rake under the roots and strained. No budging. I discovered that the cattails had grown so thick and the roots so numerous over the last few years that what lived below most of the water's surface was a many-inches-thick, spongy, nearly impenetrable mass. (For some reason, I thought of the obstructionism in the Republican party.) The spaghetti-like roots were the consistency of coir, the stiff coconut fiber often used to make rugs. It was going to take a man's strength to help me get this job done.

Andy provided the open-minded (and open-hearted) Republican muscle, but I was the one with the bright idea to get us into this garden renovating/political fundraising business, so it was only fitting that I was the one to get down into the muck. In the drained pond, I wrestled in my grassroots effort, hauling out thick, black-slime covered, stinking, sawed cattails. Then I dragged the water-logged pieces across the yard with a rake. Getting up close and personal with the beige root masses was a horror show — I kept thinking about the missing goldfish. Dead, no doubt, suffocated and then eaten by . . . roots? Oh God. I kept expecting to find a fish with roots growing through it, its dead eyes staring at me, terrified and accusing. That vision was only slightly off; I happened upon a single perfect fish skeleton, several inches long, wedged into a section of root. Queasy but curious, I took one good, long look to imprint the image on my mind.

I was sick, literally and spiritually, about the fish. (I shouldn't have let the pond go for so long, but how could I have known what was going on below the surface?) I did penance for my sins, though, by getting into the filth and smelling the reeking chunks of pond debris for a few days, until the roots had dried out and we could haul them to a yard-waste recycling center.

After conquering the pond, we focused on the final brickwork and made trips to the recyclers with truckloads of debris — tree branches, weeds, leaves, and pruned rose canes. Andy returned with loads of mulch purchased from the same place. The drop-off was free, with a donation of canned goods. Quite cleverly, this enterprise accepted yard waste donations, then chipped and composted them, then sold them right back to the people who brought the waste in! We bought mulch, sand, and roadbase for the brick laying, and I, along with Zora (who was earning money for tickets to a Nine Inch Nails concert), hauled numerous wheelbarrows of the same. The highlight of the garden's transformation, for me, was when Andy became enthusiastic a week or so before the tour, surprising me with pink sandstone gravel for garden paths. If you're a gardener, you may notice that this renovation was beginning to cost money. We wound up spending a few hundred dollars for plants, organic fertilizer, and other supplies. Not exactly chump change for us, as a family of modest means, but it was money well spent.

In the meantime, I struggled with more maddening parts of the tour, namely, finding other gardeners to participate. Beatrice thought we should keep it in our neighborhood and feature landscapes designed, planted, and maintained by their working and middle-class owners. I agreed. She convinced her next-door neighbor, a retired art teacher, to join us. I corralled Kate and Cheryl, two landscape professionals/genius garden goddesses. Kate suggested a woman I didn't know, and she agreed to be on the tour as well. That made six gardens, including Beatrice's mini-garden, but I felt we still needed one or two more.

I decided to write notes to three neighbors. "Hi, I've admired your garden for years. . . . We're doing a fundraiser for Barack Obama. . . ."

I figured a sweet, well-worded note would not put them on the spot, or on the defensive. I also found out that it didn't exactly compel them to join us. Out of three queries, the first replied, "Thanks, but we haven't made up our mind on a candidate yet." The second, which had gone to a mixed couple (one for Hillary/one for Obama, I learned from the yard signs not long after), didn't receive any response. The third, which I later discovered had gone to a hard-core Republican supporter (*oopsie!*), was politely declined. I discovered number three's political alignment from Yolanda, another Obama volunteer. She found it quite amusing. I cringed a little but got over it.

We'd make do with what we had, a decision that turned worrisome when one gardener became nearly impossible to reach. Frustrations mounted as more and more phone messages and e-mails went unanswered. Only at three weeks before the tour (and after I became snippy when she off-handedly said she probably couldn't attend our single group meeting), did we discover that she was a staunch Hillary Clinton supporter. Oh, yeah, she said she was still *in*, but she probably wouldn't need any Obama volunteers to help her on tour day. At first, my heart sank. During my work as a precinct captain for Obama at the caucus, I had seen this: Democrats behaving badly. In fact, two of the neighbors on this tour and I had witnessed a Clinton supporter "accidentally" transpose the primary results in our district, putting Obama's much higher tally under Clinton's name. When we confronted her, she apologized for the "mistake." We didn't buy that it was a mistake. Being new and naïve to the ways of politics was challenging enough . . . with this new obstacle, a split Democratic party, visiting itself upon the garden tour, an anger began to bloom in me. The previous weeks' dealings with the Hillary gardener now seemed obvious — out-and-out passive-aggressive behavior! I wanted to kick her off the tour. Fortunately, I hashed out our problem with Beatrice. With her calmer, more rational and mature demeanor, she led me to higher ground. We would make like Obama; we would play it cool. We'd work it out.

Beatrice, an artist who designed the flyer for the tour, was working with the Obama office and dealing with her own huge to-do list: finding volunteers to help us on tour day, getting the proper donation paperwork (she wound up making an 130-mile roundtrip to Denver to accomplish that), and getting a lawyer friend to create a waiver that we all hated but had to have. (Just in case someone got stung by a honey bee and dropped dead in the petunias, you know.)

Beatrice also contacted the two local newspapers, while I emailed our neighborhood paper, even though I knew it to be partisan in the other direction. (A picture of Bush, Jr. graced their office wall.) Nevertheless, I had once done some work for them for very little compensation, and I thought they would be kind enough to return a favor. Besides, this was an important neighborhood event! I wrote them a flattering email, they sent one back agreeing to help us out, everything was civilized, and then . . . they left us out of the publication. Not even a single line in the calendar section. When I contacted them, they wrote back that on deadline night they "couldn't find" our information.

The next day, Beatrice and I took to the streets. We visited a three-block stretch of Colorado Avenue, our circa 1880s Old Colorado City historic business area, in hopes of hanging a few flyers. I had the south side of the street, known in cowboy days as the "bad" side, where Old West prostitutes and saloons proliferated, and Beatrice chose the reputable north side. Both sides are almost identical now, with boutiques, restaurants, and other tourist-friendly enterprises in quaint brick buildings, but still I enviously wondered if she had chosen the better route. Halfway through, I called to see how she was doing.

"Not too well," Beatrice said. "I'm not getting too many flyers up. Three, I think. One place even told me that this is the 'Republican' side of the street!"

I had to laugh. My side, the notoriously naughty side, was proving to be very positive about Obama, even though Hillary Clinton was still in the race. Almost everyone I had spoken to had either taken a flyer or agreed to hang one up in their window.

I commiserated with Beatrice, and we went on to finish our routes. It was good to get out there, visit the people, and do some campaigning! I met a business owner who said he'd been a lifelong Republican but was now backing Obama. He'd be happy to put up a flyer. I also dished with some ladies in an art gallery, sharing with them the comment Beatrice heard about the "Republican side of the street."

"Oh, *really*," one of them said, gazing out the window in that direction. "I wonder if it was the polyester Nazi." (I wasn't sure if polyester was in reference to her clothing or wares and didn't want to ask.) The comment was Limbaugh-esque, so derisive, but I had to chuckle again, a rather bitter chuckle, as I had just suffered a partisan wound myself. Before I met these ladies, I had visited a business in which two men and one woman, sitting around a table, had looked me up and down as I presented my Obama Garden Tour spiel. I'm not sure if their smirks were about Obama, or the way I was dressed: Levis, a big butterfly print T-shirt under a hot pink cardigan, and leopard-print Converse. I guessed both, and they seemed barely able to hold back their mirth. Worse, I knew that when I left the flyer was going straight into the trash.

Yes, there were colorful experiences galore on the Garden Tour Campaign Trail! All the while I plugged away at the to-do list for my own garden. The physical work was more extensive than I imagined; such is the price of severe neglect. The blood, sweat, and tears adage rang true as all of those and more (bruises, splinters, sore muscles, etc.), materialized during those eight weeks.

Then, finally, tour day! I wanted to dance, to sing! Oh yeah, I was all fired up and ready to go! The garden looked good, really good, and within hours I'd be released from this responsibility. I could say goodbye to my worries over whether we would be able to pull all the details together, whether anyone would show up. Instead of major renovation in my garden, after today I could get by with mere maintenance!

Everything went great. The supporters, appreciative of our efforts, seemed happy to visit our gardens and inquisitive about our cultivars. I got to gab about the new projects, keeping a garden alive through drought, which plants did well with little water, and the presidential qualities of Senator Obama.

Beatrice later told me she had a few people come by to purchase tickets who weren't aware it was an Obama fundraiser (our daily paper's bad, not ours). One Republican couple said, 'Heck, we don't care. We just like gardens!' That gave her a sweet, feel-good moment. Another Republican stormed off in a huff, no doubt imagining a liberal conspiracy.

At our home, Yolanda and Zora reported that one woman drove up, got out of her car and looked over our picket fence.

"Is this one of the gardens on tour?" she asked.

"Yes," replied Yolanda. "Come on in!"

"Well," said the woman, nose in the air, "I thought it was going to be much more . . . spectacular."

She then turned around, got in her car, and left.

Oh, burn! We laughed about it when we had a break. It's a "Down to Earth" Garden Tour, lady! So much for the audacity of real life. There was no proof she was a Republican, or a Clinton supporter, but . . .

Lily, now 13 and on the porch looking after the tickets, witnessed another political statement. A truckload of young men drove by, saw the Obama sign at the top of my purple clematis-covered arbor, and one of them yelled, "Obama SUCKS!" When Lily told me about it, I found it funny. It was even funnier to see how worked up she was.

"I wanted to throw a water bottle at them!" she said.

I thanked her for her restraint. In a town where, just four years earlier, signs were being stolen out of front yards and tires were being slashed on cars with John Kerry bumper stickers (this happened to my friend Lucy, a retired third grade teacher), a mere rude comment was great progress.

For all our hard work, we wound up making six hundred dollars for the campaign. I was disappointed, but another friend, who was volunteering many, many hours for the campaign, told me that line of thinking was misguided. Six hundred dollars wasn't a bonanza, she said, but it wasn't bad for humble work-a-day folks either. We had owned it, she said. We had accomplished something for the campaign and for ourselves, and we had brought awareness in the community. Everyone who mattered came through brilliantly, including, I'm tickled to report, the Hillary Clinton supporter.

Throughout the Garden Tour project, I kept thinking about how, for me, bringing back our garden compared to the task America would face after this election. Our country needed a resurrection, and it was going to be damned hard, harder than we could imagine, getting it back into shape. We were going to have to wade through the dirty and the ugly. We had to be willing to be scratched, to sweat, to bleed, to endure ridicule and setbacks. Our transformation was going to require more than rolling up sleeves, making sacrifices, and working through conflict. It was going to require all of us coming together. The more we got together, the more we would accomplish. There wouldn't be an end in sight, either.

After the tour, exhausted, I slacked off again, and within a couple of months, my garden began, once again, to decline. Renovating and keeping a garden healthy required constant attention and constant work, and our country was no different.

We had to keep at it. We had to commit! I had no doubt that it'd be well worth it. My family enjoyed our restored garden every single day. And, more than a thing of beauty, this new garden was better and stronger than any we'd had before.

# Nectar of the Gods (and Goddesses)

My sister-in-law Victoria was in town from Portland (she and her children, Samantha and Alex, had moved there a few years before), and we decided to take a Wednesday day trip to Boulder. My interest in local foods had been growing, so I suggested tours of the Redstone Meadery and one of Boulder's biggest attractions, the Celestial Seasonings factory. Victoria was game, so the four of us — me, Victoria, Andy, and Lily (whose turn it was to skip school), headed north on a beautiful September morning.

An hour and a half later, we entered Boulder, a city similar to Colorado Springs in outward appearance — same vegetation, similar mountain backdrop — but a world apart in ideology as far as city planning. While Colorado Springs had its charms (Garden of the Gods and Pikes Peak to name the two greatest), miles of suburban sprawl, big-box retailers and heavy traffic had, over the previous two decades, disfigured our northern and eastern boundaries.

Boulder took a different approach. While the cost of living was outrageous, those who could afford to live there enjoyed many rewards, like living in a city where ugly billboards and even uglier sprawl were no-nos. Boulder was savvy when it came to quality of life; the city championed health (locally grown organic produce, outdoor exercise, alternative fuels) and seemed to care about advancing ideals that would make minimal impacts on the environment. Unfortunately, those were values that many in my home town liked to ridicule. In fact, the phrase "The People's Republic of Boulder" was often used when the subject of Boulder and its politics came up.

As a liberal hailing from a conservative city, I've always felt a little self-conscious visiting Boulder, even though I suspected that if I actually lived in Boulder, I would miss the challenge of defending my leftist principles (or, worse, see my leftist principles taken to such an extreme that they became something else entirely). Being a "ditto-head," on either side, is stifling and boring and — and, so far, I'd never been bored in Colorado Springs.

While strolling and then lunching on Pearl St. (slices of delicious pesto-artichoke pizza and bottles of Italian lemonade), we noticed that Boulderites had a unique look. While some of the young people sported lots of tattoos (Portland-style) and seemed to be of the creative bent, the majority showed minimum body-art and dressed in comfortable, plain, high-quality, and well-made (translation: expensive) clothing. And most were physically fit — the very pictures of glowing good health! Or maybe we arrived on a day when J. Crew happened to be putting together a yoga catalog. You never know. At any rate, this did nothing to help my Colorado Springs' inferiority complex.

After a tour through the Celestial Seasonings factory, a tour that I hoped, based on their magical tea box art, would be like Willy Wonka's Chocolate Factory, but was more about learning about how many tons of imported herbs and spices they used (so much for locally grown) and wearing hairnets for 45 minutes, we arrived at The Redstone Meadery. This Meadery was also far from my fantasy. I had dreamed of something semi-rural, perhaps in a converted stone barn (as the name implied), with wildflowers and bees cavorting outside. The reality was that we found Redstone on a street near a Toyota dealership, housed in a newer, one-story commercially-zoned brick building with a few other businesses. One of those businesses was an auto body shop. I didn't know whether to find it disappointing or delightfully unpretentious.

We went in and joined a half dozen other people who were there for the 1:00 P.M. tour. Owner David Myers would be our guide. David, with his long pony-tailed hair and khaki shorts, reminded me of old-school Boulder. He spoke fast, so I had to scribble fast to keep up.

# NECTAR OF THE GODS (AND GODDESSESES)

Here are my notes:

*Mead is the oldest fermented beverage. It pre-dates wine and beer by several thousand years. It's thought that mead probably came about in this way: Hunters out on the hunt, carrying their water in animal skins, would sometimes add a little honey to sweeten the water. This honey/water concoction, combined with the yeast that was naturally in the air, fermented when it was left sitting out too long. The hunters decided that — Yowza! — they liked the taste of this fermented honey-water and they liked the fact that their stomachs got a little bloated by the yeasts' nutrition. They got a full, happy, giddy feeling! MEAD WAS BORN.*

*Honey wine became an offering to the gods (like Zeus), and it was also offered during sacrifices. Since the early mead makers didn't know exactly how the honey and water actually created mead it was determined to be: A GIFT FROM THE GODS and/or NECTAR OF THE GODS!*

*Soon people began experimenting, adding grapes, adding grains. The products of those experiments diverged to create other alcoholic beverages, including wine and beer.*

*The supply and demand for honey changed a lot during the Middle Ages, when monasteries began using a lot of bees' wax for candles, and eventually, mead began to lose popularity with the general population, though it remained a staple in colder climates.*

*The Vikings drank mead, and Shakespeare referred to it in his works. The term honeymoon refers to the ancient practice of giving a newlywed couple a month's supply (one lunar cycle) of mead. During that time, it was hoped that the wife would become pregnant. Mead was thought to be beneficial in producing boy babies.*

When David said this, I looked over at Lily and we shared a discreet eye-roll. First men were the ones to discover mead, then this! I wondered why women couldn't have been the "discoverers" of mead — perhaps while they were out on a foraging expedition, or even just hanging out at the cave or hut — wouldn't it be as likely that they could leave out water and a little honey too long until it fermented?

Anywho, to continue:

*In the 21ˢᵗ century, mead was having a resurgence in the alcohol market, with small meaderies hoping to achieve the popularity that craft beers had begun to enjoy. Twenty-five years ago, only honey mead was available; now there are meads with both high and low alcohol content, sparkling meads, still meads, and meads with added fruits, herbs, etc. When this particular meadery began, it was one of only 25 – 30 nationally. Now there are around 100, and more are cropping up.*

Myers took us through the back rooms to show us their equipment. In a large garage-like space with cement floors, we saw the big stainless-steel kettles at work producing the mead. We learned the mead was pasteurized, so they did not need to use sulfites. Mead also possessed natural properties that allowed it to "keep." (At this point, Victoria whispered to me, "Honey keeps forever. They've even found it in the Egyptian tombs, three thousand years old and still edible.")

We learned that they heat only the "must" (unfermented mead), and it never boils. We got a detailed rundown of all the temperature changes, water exchanges, yeast oxygenating, etc., that occurred in mead-making. We also learned how they made carbonated mead, how they infused fruit purees/herbs/spices into some batches, and how they filtered the mead ("Anytime you filter, you strip away flavor," said David). There was also a rundown of how the honey wine was bottled, labeled, and stored — three months for the carbonated mead, nine to twelve for the high alcohol mead, and their high-end dessert mead was stored for three years.

"This is a lot more fun than the Celestial Seasonings tour," I whispered to Victoria. She nodded in agreement.

I asked how much of the honey was local, and David said the majority, around 70 percent. A huge apiary, only a few miles away, was where they acquired most of it. They used mostly berries in their flavored meads and those came from Oregon, as Colorado was not a berry-producing state. I asked about the health of the bees. Myers said he'd heard of some hive losses recently, but not a lot.

While we were all fascinated by the history, after the tour we got to the highlight of our visit, the tasting!

As Lily watched (I promised she could sample it when we got home), Victoria and I tried about nine different meads. We were glad Andy, who didn't care for alcohol, was driving so we could relax and enjoy. And it *was* naughty fun, sampling honey wine in little shot glasses in the middle of the day, one after another, barely having time to scribble notes or murmur opinions before David or his assistant would pass the next round.

I really liked several of the honey wines. I found them to be very different from my first sampling of meads the Christmas before. Those meads, in comparison, were too sweet and too simple. I chose a bottle of Juniper Mountain Honey Wine (one of the staff's top picks) to take home. It was made with seven parts orange blossom honey and two parts wildflower honey, and David recommended it specifically as a good accompaniment with curry, a dish that Zora happened to be planning for dinner that night.

What I liked most about the meadery, beyond the obvious (high quality production, award-winning honey wines, locally sourced honey) — was their creativity. They produced a honey wine flavored with plums, one with blueberries, one with vanilla beans and cinnamon sticks. Several combined honey and grapes. We got to sample a honey/beer combo made with hops, which a lot of people in our group loved but we couldn't purchase, as it was sold out.

I also liked that the whole experience was delightfully unpretentious. Yes, a medieval-style stone meadery surrounded by wildflowers and bees out in the country would be a dream, but this one worked just fine.

We left Redstone with a few bottles of tasty mead, a light buzz (hmmmm, do you think that expression comes from mead?) and the content feeling that we'd spent a pleasant and highly educational day in Boulder. That evening, Zora's curry and the juniper-infused

217

honey wine made a nice pairing, and I thought, *We may not be Boulderites, but life here can be pretty sweet.*

# Born Again

Though I'd been an avid, some would say slightly maniacal, gardener for well over a decade, this year, this drier-than-dust spring, I turned away from the eternally optimistic gardener's attitude and embraced my inner quitter. "I'm not pouring water on the garden this year," I vowed to family and friends. "I just won't do it."

I wouldn't plant thirsty heirloom tomatoes in big plastic pots. I wouldn't go nuts with exotic annual beauties that died with the first frost. I wouldn't plant new shrubs or trees and worry if they got established. This year, I would not waste my time, my money, our water. Feeding my soul with green beauty seemed foolish anyway — if Colorado Springs was going the way of Phoenix, if we'd soon be up to our asses in cactus, and it sure looked that way, why fight it? With years of drought — harsh, unyielding conditions that seemed to mirror the political and psychological aspects of our country (a Great Recession and two years with Obama and the Democrats in power had spurred no significant changes), why should I continue to care? Why should I continue to work and to hope?

So, I watched those areas in the garden that I had not replaced with drought-tolerant plants crinkle and wither, and I let them. I thought the neighbors foolish, keeping theirs on life support. Didn't they *know* it wasn't worth it? Didn't they care about the incredible waste? June eclipsed May. More sepia sleep, brown death. Although our city's watering restrictions had eased, I still watered only once a week, keeping only a few special darlings alive.

Then July came — and it rained. And it rained. I saw plants that had held on for months flourish and new ones born. In mid-July, we returned from vacation to grass tall enough to mow. A crop of healthy weeds everywhere, but more than that. Tomato plants had sprung up in the old garden plot; squash, too, big and strong. While they would not grow to maturity, they testified that life went on, without my blessing. I found a second crop of dill and Italian flat-leaf parsley to clip for summertime meals, along with marigolds, calendula, and sweet bronze fennel babies. By August, it was a whole new landscape.

On a walk, I noticed that an elderly neighbor had placed bricks around a four-foot-tall corn plant growing in his front yard. A worn aluminum lawn chair sat beside it.

One day I caught him in his front row seat.

"Nice corn you have there," I said.

He chuckled, looked up at me from beneath his sun hat. "You know, the squirrels, they plant these kernels around, then they forget about them."

I motioned to the husked, tasseled swelling above a broad leaf. "Looks like you're getting a nice ear."

He smiled. "We'll see what happens."

The old-timer was delighting in Nature's surprise. I'd seen him many times during the drought, watering his shrubs, tending to his roses. Keeping the faith. He was not a quitter.

Neither was I. By the end of September, my own drought had finally been replaced, once again, by that ever-so-pesky optimism.

I would keep believing in the future. And, this fall, I would buy bulbs. Tulips, crocus, daffodils, lilies — and more. In addition, I saw this experience as a lesson to renew my faith in our country. This fall, I would vote. I would do my part in reaching for a brighter future.

I once learned that if you cut a tulip bulb in half, you can see what's inside. You can see the embryonic leaves, in all their perfection, and you can see the tiny flower. It's all there in its perfect pale green form, waiting for the right time to grow.

# Stove Love – Part II

It was spring again, almost a decade since I wrote my first ode to the stove. The 1930s green and yellow model had been moved to the front porch, newly (but by no means perfectly) scrubbed, and awaited the next chapter of her life. We weren't sure what that would be, if we'd sell her or keep her. Andy and I are pokey, often impractical, romantics. At first, I thought I couldn't bear to part with her. Maybe, I'd use her as a potting table; I'd fill the oven and storage drawers with small clay pots and supplies. Then I thought of the economy — with two girls headed for college maybe it wasn't such a great idea to hang on to the past and to more stuff. I scouted, briefly, for possible buyers on the internet, and then became sidetracked with other concerns.

For a few days after we moved the old girl from the kitchen to the porch, I sulked. Although the new used stove was superior in almost every way, I resented her. Her plain-Jane practicality and efficiency mocked me. Less glam, less fun. I saw the new appliance as a mirror held up to my life. *You're getting old and boring and practical, Sandra. You're selling out. The romance is dwindling.*

But it had to be done, this upgrade. The old stove, like me, was showing her wear. After 20-some years in our family, the chips in her pretty yellow and green-marbled enamel had grown bigger; dings were now dime-sized, and quarter-sized pits had enlarged to silver dollars. The rusty front drawer was rustier, and the porcelain drawer pull showed more hairline cracks. Several years back, the oven door went sloppy, opening on its own at inopportune times. Baking meant adding multiple cardboard shims. The cardboard in the door became a temptation for Chancho. He would run off with it, requiring me to repeat shim procedure (grab a Celestial Seasoning box, tear off pieces, fold, and place). Andy attempted a repair of the door with some wire; it worked for a time, then didn't. We blew off dealing with it. When you're using an 80-year-old appliance, it's easy to go with the "why bother" mentality.

So, while I was bonded with this stove for over 20 years, I had been growing impatient. There's a certain charm when you're young — in driving beat up cars and dealing with the quirks of aging appliances. They're only minor irritations, and it's easy to not give too much of a damn because you've got your whole life ahead of you and things will get better, you're sure of that. But then the years fly by, and when life hasn't produced all those magical transformations that you've dreamed of (though life is still beautiful), there comes a drop in tolerance. Eighty-year-old stoves with crap doors become less charming. The sour thought that a new stove would be nice occurs to you; that it'd be real damn nice not to have to put this freaking piece of cardboard in the door every time you bake muffins! But you look at hubby and he, God knows, has enough to deal with, too — so you check the nagging.

When I was a teenager my five younger siblings and half-siblings and I would come home from school, scavenge a snack, and gather around the TV for after-school-recovery (right before get-the-chores-done-before-Mom-comes-home time.) *Gilligan's Island* and *The Brady Bunch* were our usual fare, but sometimes we'd zone out to the materialistic antics of the contestants on *The Price is Right*. We didn't really like the show, and I wondered at the over-the-top displays some contestants made when winning hopelessly boring prizes, like appliances. They'd jump up and down, some would quake — or even, if you can imagine, *cry* — at the glorious sight of a new refrigerator or washer/dryer combo, previously caressed by one of Bob Barker's lovelies.

"WTF?" wasn't in my vocabulary in the late '70s, but that was basically my reaction. Then I grew up, became a homeowner, and learned that reliable appliances were pretty nice! If you've ever experienced the joy of spending time in a laundromat with a baby, or even more fun, at a laundromat pregnant, with a toddler running around as you try to fold clothes — or if you've experienced the joys of defrosting a non-frost-free freezer with a hair dryer — you know whereof I speak.

So maybe it wasn't really old-fogey-ism, but just a natural progression of life and wisdom when a rush of excitement came upon me the night Andy told me there might be a great stove up for grabs.

"It's at a house that's being remodeled, in the Broadmoor," he explained. "The new owner doesn't want it. It's in perfect shape."

"What brand?" I asked, although a very precise picture had already formed in my mind. With big money came quality. I flashed on stoves I'd coveted over the years in decorating magazines . . . stainless steel, with badass names like Viking and Wolf. Stoves that could withstand the lightning bolts of Thor, stoves that could cook Grandma whole.

"It's stainless steel, a four burner, with an electric convection oven."

My pulse quickened. "Is it a . . ." I stammered, dared to hope, "a Viking?"

"No, some other brand." Andy told me that not all the best stoves were Viking, never mind the advertising campaigns.

I didn't know exactly what a convection oven was, but I knew this might be my dream stove. Several weeks went by. Andy negotiated with the contractor. He researched the brand, DCS — Dynamic Cooking Systems — on the internet (a very fine stove, indeed!). I held my breath. It looked like we'd probably get it, and then, no, the contractor's son wanted it. That was that. No new used stove for me.

I was disappointed, but not crushed. It didn't surprise me that they wanted to keep it. Yet it did make it more difficult to fry my eggs on the old one.

Then, two years later, another turn of events (I told you things don't happen fast around here). The contractor's son decided to sell the stove. Andy could buy it, for a pretty penny, but still a fraction of its value and less than an ordinary stove. He would pick it up in Boulder, 90 miles away.

It was weird, changing them out. Next to the 1930s beauty, this stove looked as tough and boxy as a women's prison guard. No nonsense. Black and silver. Even the name, DCS, lacked beauty.

It took three of us to get her up the front stairs and into the kitchen. My shoulder hurt for days. She was ungodly heavy. Her oven door, with its glass window, was massive and closed up tight as a safe.

At first, Zora and Lily weren't exactly thrilled with the new stove. Lily's best friend since kindergarten, Shelby, was especially disappointed. She loved the quirks of the old stove — lighting the burners and oven with a lighter, even the cardboard shim thing. She had known that stove since kindergarten; it had played a role in many summer tea parties and pancake breakfasts after sleepovers.

Our new stove had one broken knob, an injury during the first move (we'd ordered a replacement), and one of the burner sensors needed cleaning. Otherwise, she was in tip-top shape. Low mileage, one could say, as her previous owners were away most of the time. I admired the streamlined ease with which she was designed. A row of five tiny rubber buttons to push: Off, Bake, Conv (for Convection), Broil, and Light. She had four big, black burner knobs, which went from high flame to the tiniest simmer I had ever seen; a light (a light, what would they think of next!) illuminated the oven. Three tiny red lights indicated: Oven On, Heating, and Door Locked. She wasn't super fancy, not slick, but she was *so* practical. We tried her out, and it was a magnificent experience to cook with someone of her abilities.

She suited me pretty well, and I began to look past the hard-edged exterior to the inner possibilities. One night, after hours of shoveling dirt in our new community garden plots (my latest garden experiment), I drifted off to sleep at about 7:00 P.M., in front of the TV with my work clothes on. When I awoke, Ruth Reichl (food writer extraordinaire) was on some PBS show talking about gardening and food. She was showing how to oven-dry tomatoes — drying them to the point where they could be powdered. She then talked about using this wonderful tasty ingredient on pasta, deviled eggs, etc. Although I was secretly scheming to get Andy to build a solar food dehydrator, I thought, as the possibilities brought me to consciousness, *I can do that this summer with home-grown tomatoes! This would be perfect in my new oven!*

Zora immediately came around to loving the new stove. "The rice cooks better," she announced after preparing a dinner of Indian food, a once-a-week ritual she'd adopted. She was the first to bake with the new stove, making cupcakes for her classmates on her 18th birthday. They, too, were perfect. I played with the convection aspect and marveled at the speediness, the evenness, the crispness it brought to bread crusts. This new girl could cook!

What really bothered me about the stoves was the whole out-with-the-old/in-with-the-new thing. They symbolized a big change in our home. While Lily would still be home for several more years, our family was growing up, getting older, and like all transformations, ours had not been easy or painless. One of the biggest changes was the girls' teenage loss of interest in the pets we'd accumulated over the years. Four years earlier, we had given away the tropical fish. A year after that, we gave away the few remaining chickens.

That fall, Zora would leave for college. I had always thought I would not be one of "those moms," those overly sentimental women falling apart when their fledglings flew the nest. (I had arrogantly imagined those moms didn't have enough going on in their lives.) But I was wrong. I was one of those moms. An era was ending, and I tried not to dwell on it, because when I did I couldn't help but to mourn. I knew I should be joyful that I had reared two perfect young women, and I was. Yet . . .

This would be a year of work for me, getting my mind and heart around it all, moving toward acceptance. This change in stoves had reflected it all. A very pretty, loving, full-of-life-and-learning, sometimes impractical and often outrageous era had drawn to a close. I, too, had grown — into a competent, secure, happy-with-her-life, middle-aged woman. I liked myself. I was not as young or pretty, but I wasn't as flakey, inexperienced, or prone to drama either.

This new chapter in my life was one to look forward to — delicious new recipes, new work, new experiments and discoveries. I would get used to cooking on this new stove.

# Epilogue

As I put this book together and reread these stories, I discovered only one regret, a big one, which I'd like to atone for here. When I confessed to Zora and Lily that I felt uneasy about publishing one of the stories, "Please Don't Piss on the Petunias," they said I had a good reason to be uneasy. As Zora put it, "You look like an asshole in that story, Mom."

I bristled and reminded her, "It was your dad who should have stepped up with Broonzy, not me."

Then Lily added her two cents: "Mom, we know that, but you *should* have trained him."

*Sure*, I thought, *as the mother, I'm supposed to take care of everything and everyone! What a stereotypical bunch of bullshit!* But their words stuck with me.

A week later, when the subject came up again with my dog-loving neighbor and friend, Yolanda, she made the comment: "I never thought you did right by that dog."

Again, I bristled, but in this case, I laughed it off. "Well, Yolanda," I said, "you'll have to read the story. It was *complicated*." To myself I thought, *What does she know? She didn't have to deal with him.*

Then I started reading the stories again, editing them, reliving the joy, the fun, and the aggravation. By the time I finished "the Broonzy story," as we called it, the tears were flowing. Broonzy had been gone for two years (he lived to age 14). Zora and her fiancé Noel had just adopted a puppy, a German shepherd/Lab mix who was destroying much of their apartment. He had dismantled a couch and had even ripped out drywall with his teeth! Yet, on our almost daily telephone calls, Zora *laughed* about Tristan's destruction. In contrast to her joy, reading about Broonzy's life and knowing how the story ended (with me never budging and Andy never taking responsibility) brought a kind of devastation that only came with a mature realization:

227

Broonzy had a good life; he was well-loved and given ample attention, but he didn't have the life he *should* have had with us.

I poured my heart out to Zora on the phone and she comforted me. "Mom, he was just caught in the crossfire of your marriage."

Another realization then hit me, hard. Through tears, I blurted, "I was Broonzy's evil stepmother, Zora!" That thought was almost too much to bear. I'd been a stepchild to several during my life, and I knew that station in life at its worst. The truth was this: the resentfulness I felt toward my husband came out in my actions towards an innocent — Broonzy! I now saw how wrong that had been.

Well, that's my confession. And here's my apology: I am so sorry, Broonzy. If I could do it over, and do better, I would.

The only silver lining, besides my own growth through recognizing (and eventually forgiving) my assholery, is if there is someone reading this who has put his or her foot down and won't budge, someone who feels like he or she has the moral high ground in a similar situation with a dog . . . or a child, or any other innocent . . . well, I'm here to tell you: *You are better that that!* If you and your partner are decent people (and most of us are, in spite of our flaws), you can figure out how to bend and how to include that innocent being *fully* in your boundless love. Make the commitment, even if it's not easy. You won't be sorry.

On a political note: I started putting this book together in 2016, a year that will be remembered by many as the worst election year in United States history. I wasn't even sure, in early 2018, whether "The Audacity of Dirt" would make it as one of the stories because, while I supported Barack Obama in 2008 and 2012, in 2016 I was a 53-year-old "Bernie Bro" and had been disenchanted with Obama for years. If there's one thing I've learned, it's that we need to unite across party lines, across ideologies, for all the things we care about, because we are more the same than we are different, no matter what polarizing politicians, greedy oligarchs, and corporate media would have us believe. The vast majority of us care deeply about our families, our country, and the planet.

# EPILOGUE

Another revelation I had while going through these stories was discovering that the Master Gardener certification class I wrote about in the second chapter, "Mistress Gardeners," now costs an exorbitant six hundred dollars for an *online* class (compared to fifty dollars in 1997 for a classroom experience and three notebooks worth of handouts!). I love the internet as a learning tool, but there's no substitute for personal connections with teachers and other students. I hope our universities get it together on this issue, as we need as many educated horticulturalists as we can get. For those who are interested, I did find a link to pdfs for much of the Colorado coursework:

http://cmg.colostate.edu/Gardennotes/training-file.pdf

Lily made an interesting discovery when helping edit this book — there has been more research on the phenomenon of sex reversal in chickens since I wrote "My Gender Bender Hen." In fact, it is now known that ovotestes *can* produce sperm (though there has not been evidence of transformed hens siring chicks, yet). There are also reports of roosters who have undergone a sex reversal and even laid eggs (the article notes that this is extremely rare). The annotated article and podcast can be found here:

http://www.urbanchickenpodcast.com/ucp-episode-018/

One of the coolest things I experienced during two decades of exploring the "green fringe" was watching what was quirky and rare 20 years ago — raising backyard chickens — become more mainstream. That thrills me, as does the fact that our neighbors across the street are growing vegetables in their front garden and keeping bees in the back. Only two blocks away, another neighbor is raisings chickens and goats and has a large greenhouse for vegetables! More neighbors have replaced their front lawns with flowers and shrubs to feed our pollinators — and the use of glyphosate is being exposed for what it is, a serious danger to our health. People are connecting more and more with the Nature right outside their own homes, and learning to cultivate food and beauty.

As for our family, we're all doing well and have many adventures going on or planned. Chancho is still with us (he's now 12 and we dote on him every single day). After Tulio passed two years ago we rescued a rat terrier from Houston, Texas that I named . . . Eleanor (or Ellie Mae for short). I continue to garden.

The very best thing about this book, this life, is that not very long ago, Zora said to me, "I am so grateful for our childhood." Lily agreed.

I was astonished. My first thought popped out of my mouth, "But you girls didn't even get to go to Disneyland!"

They laughed.

I couldn't have wished for a happier ending.

# Acknowledgments

Everyone (animal, vegetable, and mineral) who appears in this book helped create this book. Thank you all.

I am especially indebted to my beta readers: Sandy Poney, Virginia Gambardella, Frances Dunn, Freida Pearce, Lurene Connor and Maurya K. Orr.

Zora and Lily Knauf, Cheri Colburn, and Sandy Poney went above and beyond in their editing input. And, as usual, my right-hand woman, Zora, came through in many other ways; formatting, dealing with all the publishing requirements, and keeping me on track when I didn't think I could bear another rewrite. Once again, I could not have done it without you.

Last, but not least, thank you, dear Andy. I could not have created this beautiful life without you.

# About the Author

Sandra Knauf is the owner of Greenwoman Publishing. Her books include the six-volume series *Greenwoman* (compilations of literary garden writing and art, with many contributors); her YA environmental fantasy novel, *Zera and the Green Man*; and *Fifty Shades of Green*, an anthology of erotic gardening stories that she describes as "the feminist-gardener answer to *Fifty Shades of Grey*."

Sandra was a 2008-09 featured "Colorado Voices" columnist for *The Denver Post* and her humorous essays have appeared nationally in *GreenPrints* and *MaryJanesFarm*, as well as many local publications. She's also been a guest commentator on KRCC's (NPR's southern Colorado affiliate station) *Western Skies* radio show.

Sandra lives in Colorado Springs, Colorado with her family, dogs, a huge organic urban garden, and lots of books.

Thank you for reading *Please Don't Piss on the Petunias: Stories About Raising Kids, Crops, and Critters in the City*. If you enjoyed this book, please consider leaving a review at Amazon.com or Goodreads, and/or asking your local library to purchase a copy.

My publishing company, Greenwoman Publishing, LLC, also offers a newsletter. If you'd like to keep updated on other books and receive information on discounts and contests to win free books and prizes, please visit www.greenwomanpublishing.com.

Sincerely,

Sandra Knauf

Made in the USA
San Bernardino, CA
25 January 2019